Patterns for Costume Accessories

by Arnold S. Levine
& Robin L. McGee

Costume & Fashion Press

an imprint of
Quite Specific Media Group, Ltd.
Hollywood

First published 2006
© 2006 by Arnold S. Levine and Robin L. McGee

Costume & Fashion Press
an imprint of
Quite Specific Media Group Ltd.
7373 Pyramid Place
Hollywood, CA 90046

(323) 851-5797 v. (323) 851-5798 f.
Email: info@quitespecificmedia.com

ISBN 0-89676-241-6

Quite Specific Media Group Ltd. imprints:
Costume & Fashion Press
Drama Publishers
Jade Rabbit
EntertainmentPro
By Design Press

www.quitespecificmedia.com

Contents

Acknowledgments

The patterns in this book are the result of years of working in the costume shops of various theaters across the country. Our thanks go to all of the designers whom we have worked with and for, to all the pattern makers and drapers who have let us in on their secrets and to the craftspeople who have shared techniques and resources. We thank our friends who thought that this book was a good idea and would make a useful tool and who shared our excitement when things were going along smoothly and commiserated when we were bogged down. Thank you to those who listened while we argued about whether the instructions made sense. "What does this mean?" "Do you really do it that way?"

Thanks to the teachers who tried to teach us geometry. "If we knew that what we were going to do with our lives involved so much math, we might have paid more attention." And thanks to all the teachers who have influenced and guided us through the years.

We also thank our families who always knew we could do it and gave us the "Big Yes" and let us try.

Robin would like to specifically thank: Arnold Levine, my partner in this endeavor; Gail and Joe McGee for never saying that getting a degree in theater was crazy, even though they thought so, and for their unwavering support; Carol Lancet, Susan Tsu and all of those at University of Texas; Mike Hanes—an inspiration; Karen Hart—an outstanding friend; my New York "family" for their love and support; and Lisa Kiraly for talking me into auditioning for my first play as a freshman in high school.

Arnold would like to specifically thank: Richard Storm for putting up with all of it; Cigmond Meachen who puts up with most of it; my friends and faculty from Carnegie-Mellon University; Cletus Anderson who made me want to be a costume designer; Barbara Anderson who showed that pattern drafting is logical and beautiful—the more you refine a pattern, the more simple the shapes become; and Robin McGee who one day casually asked if I would like to help her with a book she was "thinking about." Now years later, *voila*.

Techniques

Techniques _____

This book presents patterns for those costume accessories that keep appearing in the various staged productions we have worked on over the years. We have included basic shapes and styles, and as you become familiar with the patterns and techniques you will be able to mix, match, and alter the basics to create any needed variations. Feel free to manipulate the patterns, add trims, or otherwise change them to suit your needs. Have fun.

General Instructions

Before you begin, obtain an accurate and complete set of measurements for the actor. In certain instances, special or out of the ordinary measurements will be needed. You should read the instructions for the pattern prior to measuring the actor and make a complete list of measurements needed.

1. The patterns are laid out on a grid; each square on that grid is equal to one inch. To enlarge the patterns to the proper size, you can use one of two methods. You may either carefully draw the pattern onto one inch grid paper or you may take the pattern to a photocopying machine and enlarge the pattern until the grid equals one inch. Patterns are presented in one of four ways: actual size, 50% actual size, 25% actual size, or ⅛ actual size. If you are working in centimeters, simply use the pattern as is or enlarge it two, four, or eight times, depending on the presentation. We should add, 1 inch equals 2.54 centimeters. To figure the measurements in centimeters, multiply the number of inches by 2.54.

2. After the pattern has been enlarged to the proper size, it should be checked against the actor's measurements and adjusted as necessary.

3. Seam allowances are not included on these patterns. You should now add seam allowance to your pattern by drawing the desired depth around the outer edge of each pattern piece, according to your personal preference.

4. For the best fit and final product, it is suggested that a "mock-up" of the pattern be made first in a fabric similar to what will be used in the final construction. Making a "mock-up" will allow the costumer to discover any changes that need to be made to the pattern.

5. Fit the "mock-up" on the actor. Be attentive to the fit of the garment not only while the actor is standing still but also while the actor is in motion, checking that it does not impede their

movement. Make note of any design or construction changes you wish to make at this point as well.

6. Adjust the pattern (if necessary) and construct the item in the final materials.

7. Fit on the actor again if time allows. This will enable you to double check the item and make any additional changes or corrections necessary.

General Pattern Instructions

1. Enlarge pattern pieces as described above.
2. Add seam allowance as necessary.
3. Lay the pattern on the fabric, placing grain line indicator on the straight grain of fabric.
4. Cut out pieces. Make sure you transfer all marks on pattern to the wrong side of the pieces.

Basic Techniques

Topstitching

Topstitching is machine stitching that runs parallel and usually close to the seam or edge. It is stitched from the right side of the garment.

The most important thing to remember about topstitching is that it will be seen. If you do not want to see it, don't do it. Topstitching is used in construction to help re-enforce and strengthen seams and to emphasize structural lines. On baseball caps, topstitching is a basic part of the look of the item. Topstitching can be used to control edges that might otherwise have a tendency to roll or be lumpy, for example around cuffs or collars.

The easiest way to do topstitching is to line the seam or the edge of the piece against the edge of the presser foot of the sewing machine. Then just allow the foot to determine the depth of the topstitching. Additional lines of topstitching may be added—just be very careful to keep them parallel to the first line.

Clipping Corners and Curves

To eliminate bulk and keep seams and edges from bulging, it is necessary to clip into seam allowances along curves and at corners. Clip only as much as necessary. Do not overclip.

For an outward curve (such as that on a sleeve cap), cut small notches or wedges into the seam allowance, being careful not to clip into the stitching. The more extreme the curve, the more you will need to notch. For a gentler curve, the notches will be smaller and/or farther apart. On an inward curve such as an underarm seam, clip straight into the seam allowance at regular intervals. **Warning:** Once a seam has been clipped or notched you cannot let the garment out. Be sure everything is correct before you clip.

Trimming Seam Allowances

Seam allowances should be trimmed only when less bulk is desired. For corners of an enclosed seam (such as the points of a collar) trim across the point of the corner close to the seamline. Then trim diagonally along each side to eliminate any bulk when the item is turned right-side out.

Chapter 1

HATS

Night Cap/Santa Hat

This simple pattern can be used for many purposes. Constructed without trim it is a night cap, worn to bed to keep the head warm or hair in place. It would be appropriate for Scrooge in *A Christmas Carol*. With the addition of fur trim, this pattern can be used for Santa Claus in your Christmas pageant.

Fabric Suggestions

- Medium weight woven or knit

Materials

- ⅝ yard fabric
- ⅔ yard ½" elastic
- 3" tassel
- ¼ yard fur (Variation #2)
- ¼ yard lining (Variation #2)
- pompon (Variation #2)

Pattern Pieces

- Base (cut 1)
- Plain cuff, optional (cut 1 for Variation #1)
- Fur cuff, optional (cut 1 fur and 1 lining for Variation #2)

Construction

- Following the instructions on page 3, enlarge pattern pieces and cut.

Plain Cap

- Pin tassel into place as indicated on pattern.
- With right sides together, lay tassel onto hat base and stitch side seam, being sure to stitch end of tassel. Press seam open.
- Turn hem up ¾ inch to the inside of the hat, and stitch ½ inch from bottom, leaving an opening to insert the elastic. Carefully thread elastic through the hem. Overlap ends of elastic and stitch together.
- Hand stitch the opening closed.

Variation #1 with Plain Cuff or Bottom Band

- Proceed as above but do not hem.
- With right sides together, sew the center back seam of cuff. Press open.
- Fold cuff in half, right side out, matching bottom edges.
- Stitch raw edges of cuff together. Insert the cuff into opening of hat (cuff is against wrong side of hat), matching raw edges. Stitch.
- Flip cuff to outside and up onto hat. Tack in place if desired.

Variation #2 with Fur Cuff (Santa Hat)

- Proceed as above, eliminating tassel, but do not hem.
- With right sides together, sew the center back seam of cuff. Press open. Repeat with lining. **Note:** To accommodate the thickness of the fur, this cuff is lined rather than folded in half.

- With right sides together stitch lining to cuff along top edge. Turn and press. Match bottom edges and stitch raw edges together.
- Insert the cuff into opening of hat (the fur is against the wrong side of the hat), matching raw edges. Stitch.
- Flip cuff to outside and up onto hat.
- Hand stitch a pompon to the tip of the hat.

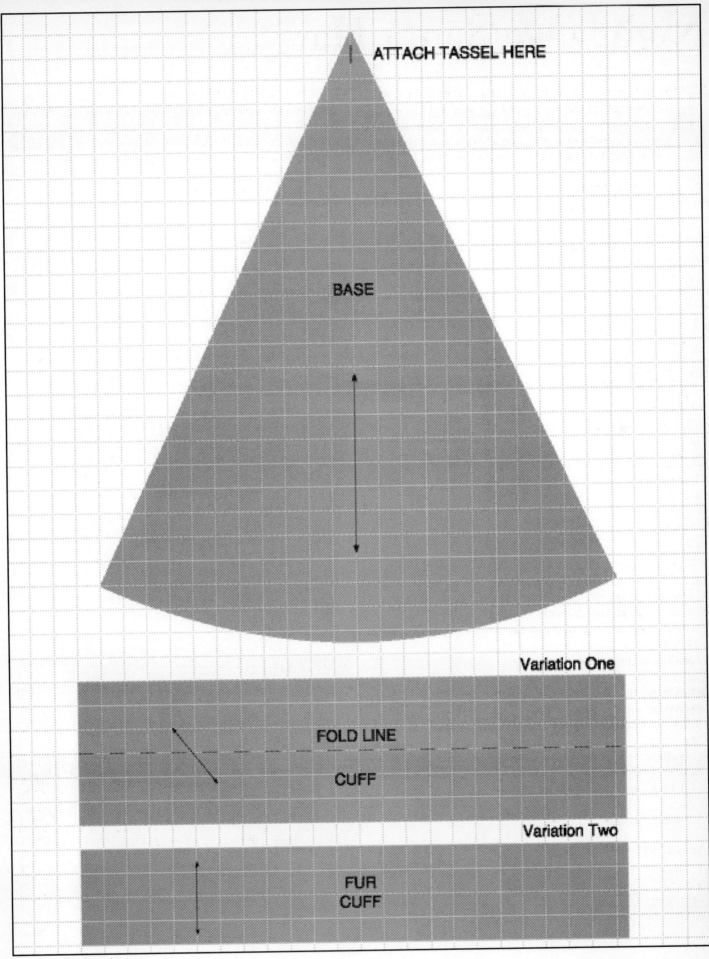

ATTACH TASSEL HERE

BASE

Variation One

FOLD LINE

CUFF

Variation Two

FUR
CUFF

Pattern is 25% of actual size.

Mob Cap

A mob cap is a woman's cap or headdress with full crown, usually soft, often with a ruffle edge. Traditionally worn by servants and other members of the working classes, these caps became fashionable during the 1700s when they were made of fancy and expensive fabrics. This pattern would be appropriate for an everyday mob cap in the mid 1700s. It can also be used as a maid's cap well into the 20th century.

Variation #1 has an even ruffle around the cap. Variation #2 has a ruffle that is shorter in the front and gets longer in the back (a Charlotte Corday Cap).

Fabric Suggestions

- Lightweight woven fabrics such as organdy, organza, sheer linen or cotton.

Materials

- ¾ yard fabric
- 2½ yards lace or trim for edging (up to 1½ " wide), optional
- 1¼ yard 1" single-fold bias tape
- ⅔ yd ¾" elastic

Pattern Pieces

- Crown (cut 1)

Construction

- Following the instructions on page 3, enlarge pattern piece and cut.
- Lightly trace casing line onto fabric. Stitch bias tape to casing line, folding cut ends under to leave an opening for the elastic.
- Hem or trim outside edge as desired.
- Thread elastic through casing.
- After checking elastic length for fit, overlap ends of elastic and stitch.
- Trim as desired, perhaps with ribbons, bows, or flowers.

Note: Simply move the casing line to change the proportion of the ruffle to the crown.

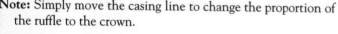

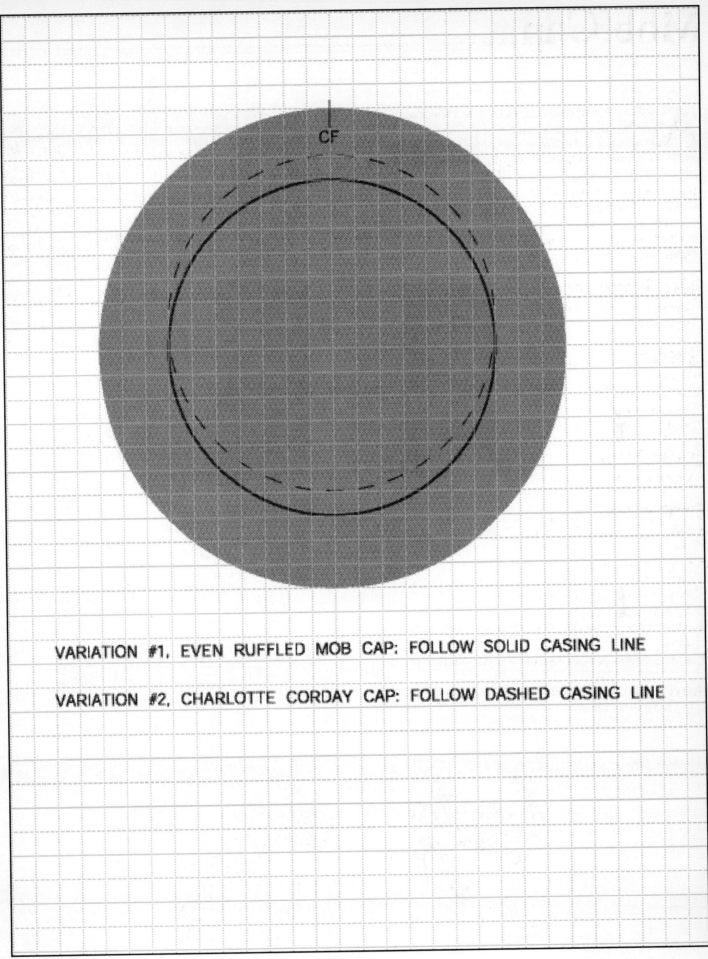

CF

VARIATION #1, EVEN RUFFLED MOB CAP: FOLLOW SOLID CASING LINE

VARIATION #2, CHARLOTTE CORDAY CAP: FOLLOW DASHED CASING LINE

Pattern is ⅛ actual size.

Chef's Hat

A chef's hat is worn by chefs and others in the food service business and is usually a band with a larger circular piece on top. Use this pattern for a play that takes place in a restaurant or that has an array of household servants such as *She Stoops to Conquer*, *The Taming of the Shrew*, or *The Would-Be Gentleman*. This pattern is adjustable.

Fabric Suggestions

• Twill, sturdy cotton or cotton blend.

Materials

• 1 yard fabric
• 6" matching ½" single-fold bias tape
• 2" piece of 1" Velcro

Pattern Pieces

• Crown (cut 1)
• Band (cut 2)

Construction

• Following the instructions on page 3, enlarge pattern pieces and cut.
• With right sides together, stitch around bottom edge and two short sides of base pieces, leaving the top edge open. Clip corners, turn right side out and press.
• Clip crown where marked and bind the slit with matching bias tape. Press.
• Starting at the bound slit, sew a gathering thread around the outside of the circle.
• Gather the crown to fit the band.
• With right sides together, line the slit up with the ends of the band and pin crown to top, outside edge of band. Stich, being sure to sew through outside of band only (not both edges).
• Fold down all seam allowances into the band, enclosing the raw edges. Stitch.
• Topstitch around all sides of band if desired.
• Attach Velcro where indicated. Attach the loop (soft) side of the Velcro to the insice of the hat and the hook (rough) side of the Velcro to the outside of the hat.

Costume sketch by Robin McGee for Caesar the Clown in Ringling Brothers & Barnum & Bailey Circus 130th Edition Adventure.

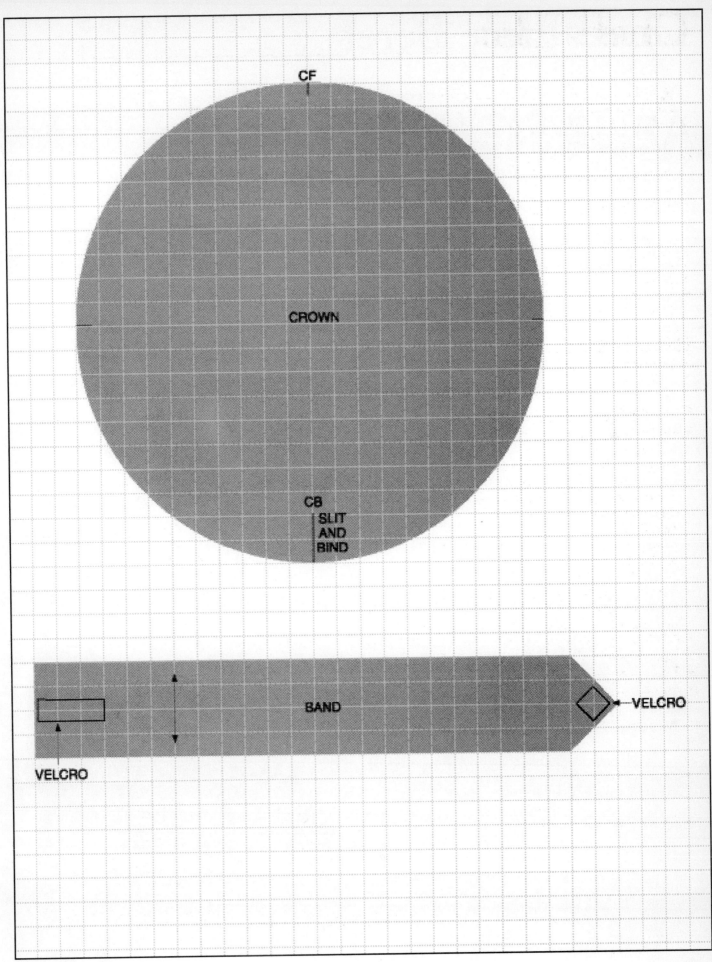

CF

CROWN

CB
SLIT
AND
BIND

BAND

VELCRO

VELCRO

Pattern is 25% actual size.

Three-Piece Beret

A beret is a visorless, usually woolen, cap with a tight head-band and a soft, full flat top. This pattern is a round soft cap adapted from a Basque beret. Variations of this hat are worn by the British, French and Russian Navies. When made in wool with a plaid band it is a Balmoral Bonnet worn in Scotland. Made with plaid wool and a pompon on top it is a Tam-o'-shanter. This beret fits a 23½ inch head—adjust as necessary.

Fabric Suggestions

- Nearly any fabric (but nothing too light weight) would be suitable for this pattern depending on use—wool, melton, canvas or denim.

Materials

- ½ yard fabric
- ⅛ yard interfacing (variation #1)
- 23½" (plus seam allowance) grosgrain ribbon or petersham (variation #2)

Pattern Pieces

- side crown (cut 2)
- tip (cut 1)
- band: 3" × 23½" plus seam allowance (cut 1 for variation #1)

Construction

- Following the instructions on page 3, enlarge pattern pieces and cut.
- With right sides of side crown pieces together, sew side seams. Press seams open and topstitch.
- With right sides together, stitch tip to crown. Clip curve, turn and press seams open. Topstitch.

Variation #1 with Band

- If fabric needs stiffening, attach interfacing to wrong side of band. Sew center back seam of band. Press seam open and top-stitch.
- With right sides together, stitch band to base of crown. Clip curve and press seam allowances toward band.
- Fold seam allowance of raw edge of band to wrong side of band. Pin this folded edge to seam line of crown and band, enclosing seam allowances.
- Hand stitch in place. Topstitch band if desired.

Variation #2 without Band

- Cut a piece of grosgrain ribbon or petersham to fit the actor's head plus seam allowances. Fold back one seam allowance.
- Sew grosgrain ribbon to bottom edge of crown, aligning the top edge of the ribbon with the inner edge of the seam allowance. Overlap folded-back edge of grosgrain over raw edge. Turn to inside of hat and press.

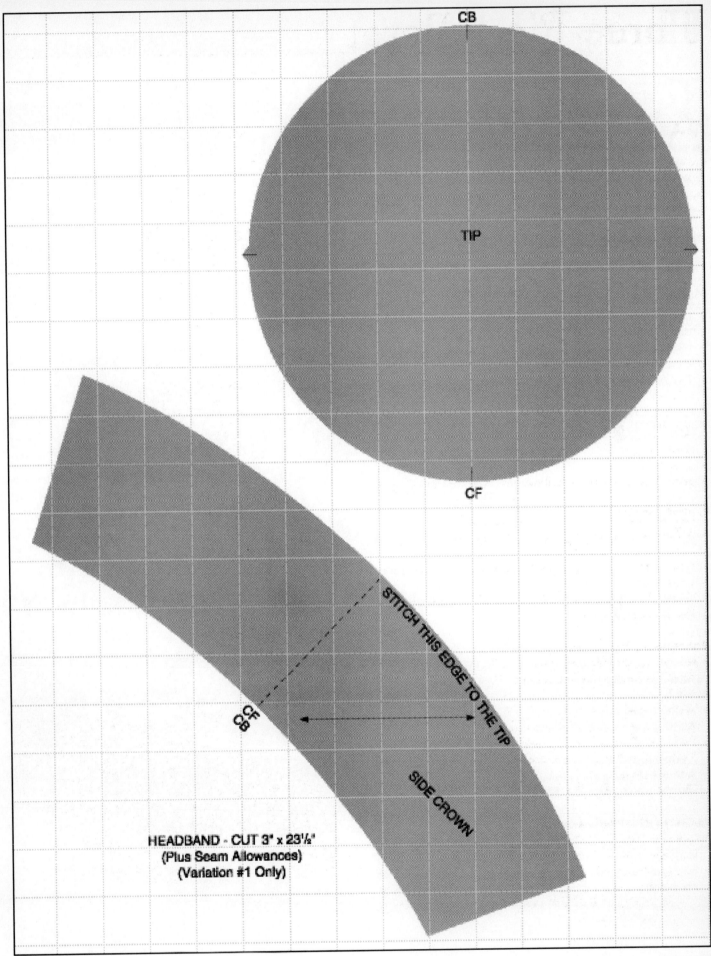

CB

TIP

CF

STITCH THIS EDGE TO THE TIP

CF
CB

SIDE CROWN

HEADBAND - CUT 3" x 23½"
(Plus Seam Allowances)
(Variation #1 Only)

Pattern is 50% actual size.

Henry VIII Hat

The Henry VIII hat, named for the hat worn by the British monarch, was at its height of popularity in the first half of the 1500s. We begin to see the hat in research as early as the 1400s and we continue to see it as a hat worn by the common people until the mid 1600s. Appropriately, this hat would be used in any play about Henry VIII, and it can find its way into most Shakespeare plays. This is also a staple hat for many opera choruses. You can refer to portraits and other art of the period for trimming inspiration.

Fabric Suggestions

- Velvet, rich brocade, upholstery fabric.

Materials

- 1 yard face fabric
- 1 yard lining
- 1 yard interfacing, optional depending on weight of fabric
- ¾ yard grosgrain ribbon #5 (⅞ " wide)
- Trims and feathers, optional

Pattern Pieces

- Brim (cut 2)
- Crown (cut 1)

Construction

- Following the instructions on page 3, enlarge pattern pieces and cut.
- If your face fabric is thin or more body is desired, attach a layer of interfacing to the wrong side.
- With right sides together, stitch back seam of brim. Repeat with second piece.
- Pin brim pieces right sides together, matching center back seams. Stitch outside edge. Clip curves, turn and press.
- Topstitch or trim outer edge as desired.
- Baste the two layers of the brim together around the inside edge.

Variation #1—Gathered Crown

- Stitch two rows of gathering stitches around the circumference of the crown piece.
- With the right side of the crown against the wrong side of the brim, pin the quarter marks on the crown to the quarter marks on the brim.
- Pull threads and gather crown to the size of the brim, making sure the gathers are even. Pin in place. Stitch.

Variation #2—Pleated Crown

Pleating the crown will give a flatter appearance to the hat.
- With the right side of the crown against the wrong side of the brim, pin the quarter marks on the crown to the quarter marks on the brim.

- Make a 1-inch pleat on either side of the quarter pins. Make second pleats next to each of the first pleats. Continue around the hat until all the crown fabric has been pleated into the brim. Stitch.

Both Versions

- Cut a piece of grosgrain ribbon to fit the actor's head plus seam allowance. Fold back one seam allowance. Pin ribbon to seam allowance of brim, matching top edge of ribbon to the previously sewn seam. Hand or machine stitch in place.
- Fold ribbon up into cap. Press to hold into position. This will cover the seam allowances.
- Shape brim as desired—up, down, curled, etc.
- Add plumes and trims as desired.

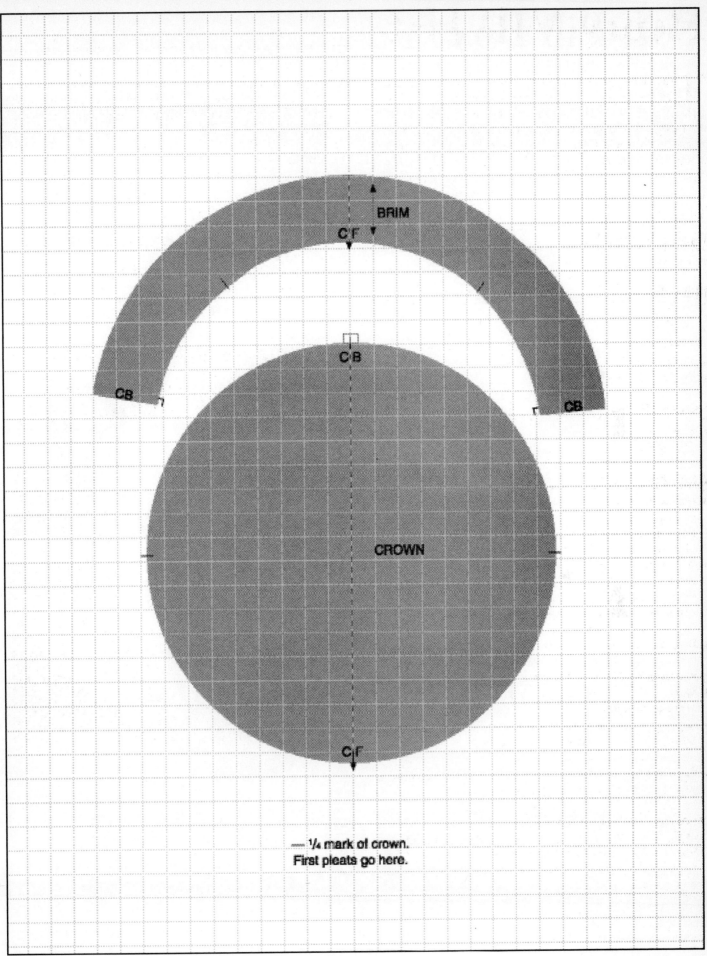

BRIM

C F

C B

CB

CB

CROWN

C F

—— ¼ mark of crown.
First pleats go here.

Soft Pill Box

Pill box caps have straight sides and flat tops, named because they resemble a box for holding pills. These hats came into fashion during the 1930s but regained popularity in the early 1960s when Jackie Kennedy, First Lady of the United States, wore them with such flair. This pattern can also be used for bell hops, ushers and chain-gang member or prisoners. Made out of a fancier fabric with a tassel on top, you would have a man's smoking cap.

Fabric Suggestions

- Almost any fabric can be used, depending on the desired effect, as long as it can be turned right side out after sewing.

Materials

- ⅓ yard face fabric
- ⅓ yard lining fabric
- ⅓ yard interfacing (optional)

Pattern Pieces

- Side (cut 1 fabric and 1 lining)
- Tip (cut 1 of fabric and 1 of lining)

Construction

- Following the instructions on page 3, enlarge pattern pieces and cut.
- Sides: With right sides together, stitch the center back seam of side in face fabric. Repeat with lining.

- With right sides together, stitch bottom edges of face and lining side pieces. Press seam allowances to the lining side. Turn right side out. Baste edges together.
- Tip: Baste (flat line) the face fabric tip to the lining tip around top edge at the stitch line. Matching the center back seam to center back notch of the tip, pin sides to the tip. Stitch.
- Bind or overlock raw seam allowances if desired. Turn hat right side out.

Notes: If you want more body, use interfacing with both pattern pieces. You may want to pipe either the top edge, the bottom edge, or both. The piping will give the hat a little more support.

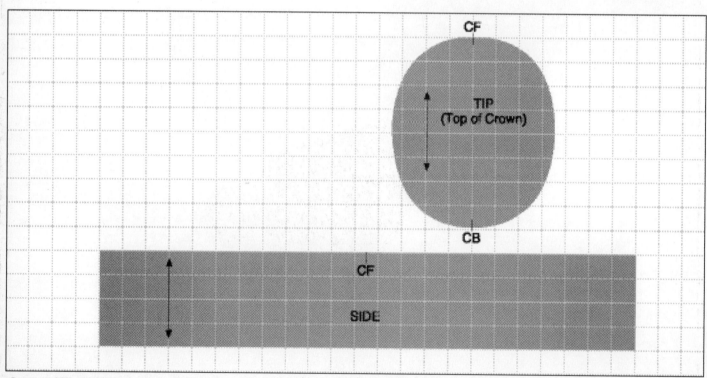

Pattern is 25% actual size.

Beanie

A beanie is small round tight-fitting skullcap worn especially by schoolboys and college freshmen. The beanie shape can be used for a yarmulke, a cardinal's cap, a calotte, a choirboys cap or a Juliet cap. This is a good basic crown with many uses. As a yarmulke it can be used in *The Merchant of Venice*; as a cardinal's cap it can be used in *The Three Musketeers* or *The Devils*.

Fabric Suggestions

- Felt, twill, or any medium weight woven fabric

Materials

- ¼ yard fabric
- ⅔ yard ½" single-fold bias binding

Pattern Pieces

- Crown (cut 6)

Construction

- Following the instructions on page 3, enlarge pattern pieces and cut.
- With right sides together, stitch two pieces together. Clip curve. Press seam allowance open.
- Stitch a third piece to first two. Clip curve and press seam allowance open. Repeat process with remaining three pieces.
- With right sides together, stitch first three pieces to second three pieces, aligning points. Clip curve and press seam allowance open.
- Bias bind bottom edge.

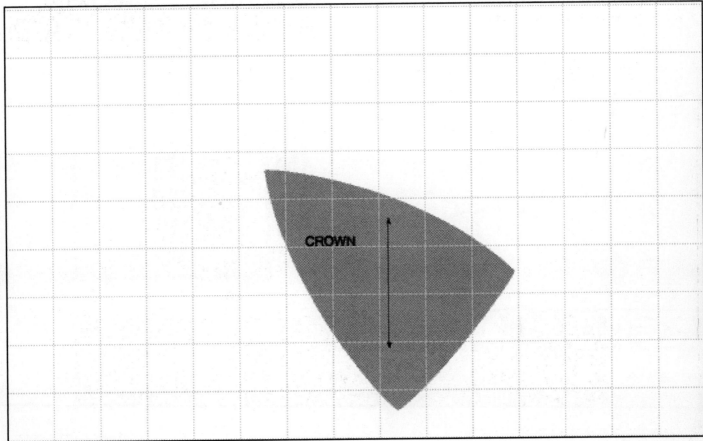

CROWN

Pattern is 50% actual size.

Baseball Cap

This is the cap worn by players in a game of baseball. It is usually made of a six piece crown with a button on top and a stiff visor in the front to shield the eyes from the sun. The game of baseball was invented in 1815, but the fashion of wearing baseball caps off the field began in the 1950s and was very popular during the 1990s. This cap is perfect for your production of *Damn Yankees,* or *Brighton Beach Memoirs.*

Fabric Suggestions

- Felt, denim, twill, or any medium weight woven fabric

Materials

- ½ yard fabric
- double buckram, cardboard or visor board for visor
- covered button
- ⅔ yard grosgrain ribbon (#5) or petersham (⅞" wide)

Pattern Pieces

- Crown (cut 6 fabric)
- Visor (cut 2 fabric with seam allowances, and 1 board without seam allowances.

Construction

- Following the instructions on page 3, enlarge pattern pieces and cut.
- *Crown:* With right sides together, stitch two pieces together. Clip curve and press seam allowance open. Top stitch on either side of the seam.
- Stitch a third piece to first two. Clip curve and press seam allowance open. Topstitch. Repeat process with remaining three pieces.
- With right sides together, stitch first three pieces to second three pieces, aligning points. Clip curve and press seam allowance open. Topstitch.

- *Visor:* With right sides together, stitch around front edge of visor cover pieces. Clip curves and turn.
- Slip visor board into cover fabric, putting all seam allowances toward one side of board, which will become the bottom side of visor. Smoothing the fabric gently towards opening, pin seam allowances together and baste close to visor. Topstitch ½ inch from outside edge. Topstitch again ¼ inch in from first topstitching line. Stitch as many lines as desired.
- With right sides together, match center front of cap to center of visor. Pin out from center. Stitch visor to cap.
- Cut a piece of grosgrain ribbon or petersham to fit the actor's head plus seam allowance. Fold back one seam allowance. Pin ribbon to bottom edge seam allowance, matching edge of ribbon to inner edge of seam allowance. Hand or machine stitch. (It is difficult to machine stitch the ribbon to the cap where the visor is attached. Stitch the ribbon to the seam allowance of the cap, not stitching through the outside of the cap.)
- Fold ribbon up into cap; this will cover all raw edges. Press to hold in position.
- Attach covered button to top of hat.

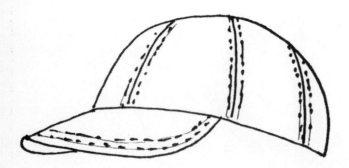

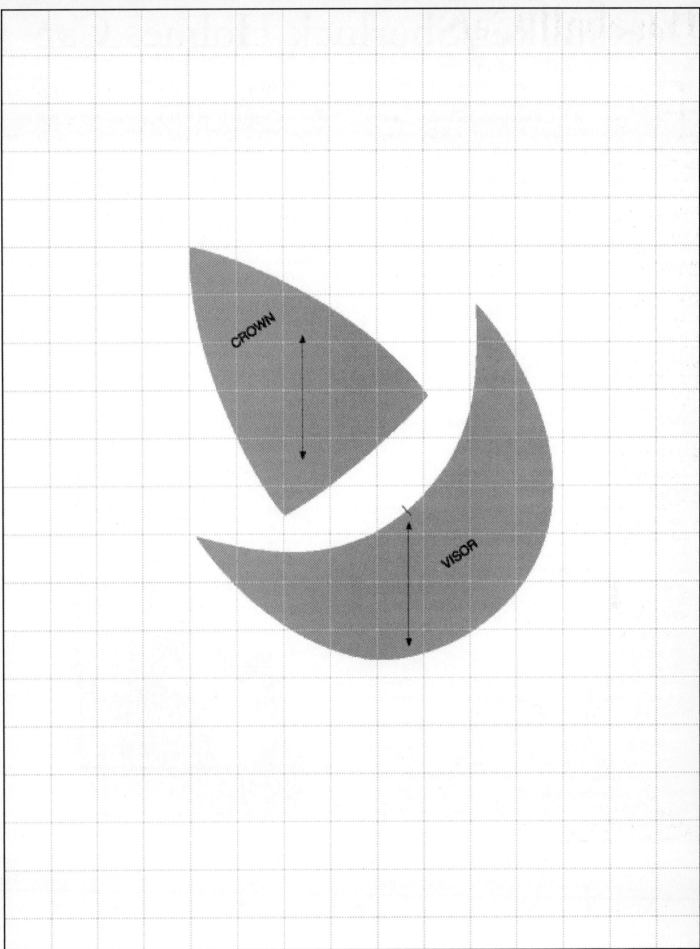

Pattern is 50% actual size.

Deerstalker/Sherlock Holmes Cap__
(Sometimes called a Fore-n-aft Cap)

The deerstalker cap has visors in front and back, and usually tear flaps that can be tied on top of head. While originally worn for hunting, it became associated with the detective Sherlock Holmes. Never mentioned in the stories, the deerstalker was drawn into the original Sherlock Holmes illustrations by Sidney Paget and later popularized in the movie versions with Basil Rathbone.

Fabric Suggestions

- Sturdy wool coatings, tweeds, glen plaids

Materials

- 1 yard wool fabric
- ¼ yard lining
- ½ yard ribbon for ties (½" wide)
- Visor board, buckram or cardboard
- ⅔ yard grosgrain ribbon (#5) or petersham (⅞" wide)

Pattern Pieces

- Crown (cut 6)
- Ear flaps (cut 2 fabric and 2 lining)
- Visor (cut 4 fabric and 2 visor board)

Construction

- Following the instructions on page 3, enlarge pattern pieces and cut.
- *Crown:* With right sides together, stitch two pieces together. Clip curve and press seam allowance open.
- Stitch a third piece to first two. Clip curve and press seam allowance open. Repeat process with remaining three pieces.
- With right sides together, stitch first three pieces to second three pieces, aligning points. Clip curve and press seam allowance open. Topstitch if desired.
- *Earflaps:* Cut ribbon into two 9" pieces. Pin a ribbon tie to the center top of ear flap piece at notch. With right sides together, sew lining to face fabric along curved outside seam, being sure to catch end of ribbon tie in seam. Clip curves, turn right sides out and press. Ribbon will now be extending out of the ear flap.
- Lay ear flaps, right side up, on each side of hat crown, carefully aligning center of earflap on the side seam. (Both ear flaps and crown should be right side out.) Baste along bottom edge of ear flap to crown stitching within the seam allowance.
- *Visors:* With right sides together, stitch around front edge of visor cover and lining. Clip curves and turn.

- Slip visor board into cover fabric placing the sewn edge seam allowance toward the lining side; this will become the visor's bottom side.
- Smoothing fabric gently toward the opening, pin the seam allowances together and baste close to the visor board. Topstitch outside edge of visor, through all layers. Repeat with second visor.
- With right sides together, match the center front and center back of cap with the center line of each visor piece. Pin in place. Stitch visors to cap.
- Cut a piece of grosgrain ribbon or petersham to fit the actor's head plus seam allowances. Fold back one seam allowance. Pin ribbon to bottom edge seam allowance, matching upper edge of ribbon to inner edge of seam allowance. Hand or machine stitch. (It is difficult to machine stitch the ribbon to the cap where the visor is attached.)
- Fold ribbon up into cap; this will cover all raw edges. Press to hold in position. Tie the ear flaps to each other over the top of the head.

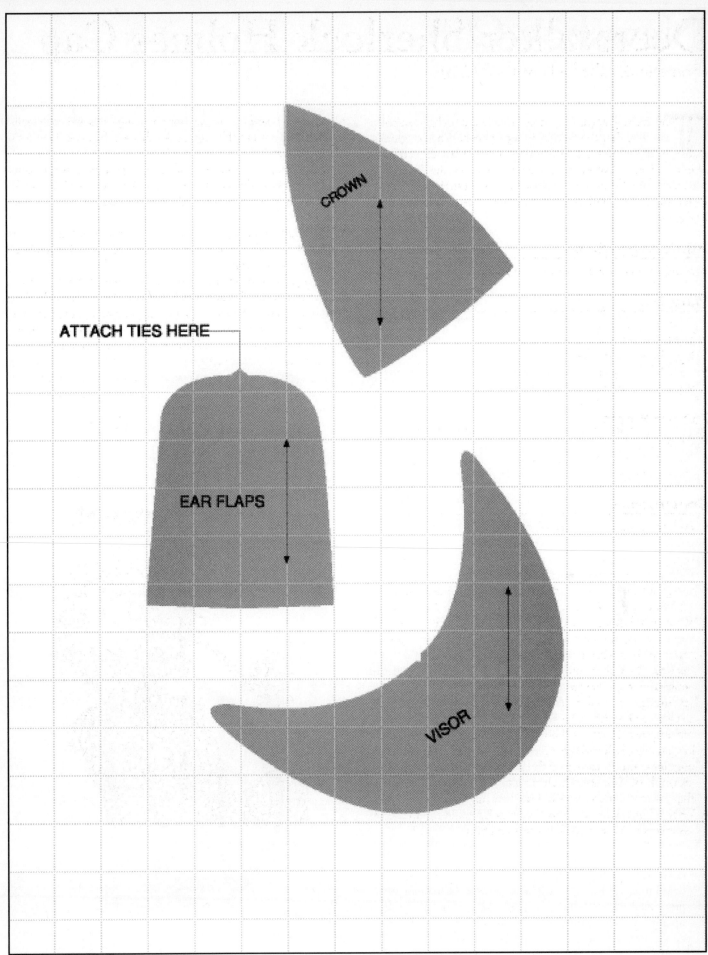

CROWN

ATTACH TIES HERE

EAR FLAPS

VISOR

Pattern is 50% actual size.

Newsboy Cap

This cap has a large pieced crown and a small visor. It is named for the cap typically worn by boys who sold newspapers around the turn of the 20th century. It was worn by the working class and sportsmen through the first half of the century. In a larger scale version they came back into style in the late 1960s. This pattern is perfect for the newsboys in *Gypsy*.

We have included two versions of the cap: one with a six-section crown and one with an eight-section crown. The cap with the six-section crown is more angular and is the version that was popular in the 1970s, while both versions were worn during the 1920s.

Fabric Suggestions

• Wool, corduroy, knit

Materials

• ¼ yard face fabric
• ¼ yard lining, optional
• Buckram or cardboard for visor
• ⅔ yard grosgrain ribbon #5 or ⅞" petersham
• 1 self covered button

Pattern Pieces

• Crown (cut 6 or 8 fabric and 6 or 8 lining, depening on style)
• Visor (cut 2 fabric with seam allowances and 1 board without seam allowance

Construction

• Following the instructions on page 3, enlarge pattern pieces and cut.
• *8-section crown:* With right sides together, sew two pieces together. Repeat this with the other pieces so you end up with four quarters. Press seam allowances open. With right sides together, sew two quarters together, forming a half. Repeat with other two quarters. Press seam allowances open.
• *6-section crown:* With right sides together, sew two pieces together. Press seam allowance open. Add another section, being sure to align the points at the top of the crown, forming a half. Repeat with other three sections.
• *Both crowns:* With right sides together sew the two halves together. Press seam allowances open.
• *Lining:* Assemble the lining, repeating the steps above. Slip lining into cap, wrong sides together, matching seams. Stitch around bottom edge within seam allowances.
• *Visor:* With right sides together, stitch outside curve of visor cover pieces. Clip curve. Turn and press. Slip visor board into cover fabric, putting all seam allowances toward the side of the board that will become the bottom side of the visor. Smoothing the fabric gently toward opening, pin seam allowance of opening tightly against the visor and baste. Topstitch outer curve of visor. Line up center front of cap with the centerline

of visor. Pin in place. Stitch close to visor material using a zipper foot.
• Cut a length of grosgrain ribbon or petersham to the actor's head size plus seam allowance. Fold back one seam allowance. Pin the ribbon to the bottom edge of the cap, matching the top edge of the ribbon with the inner edge of the cap seam allowance. Stitch in place. Turn up ribbon to cover raw edges and press in place.
• Attach covered button to top of cap.

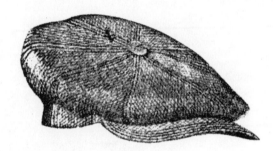

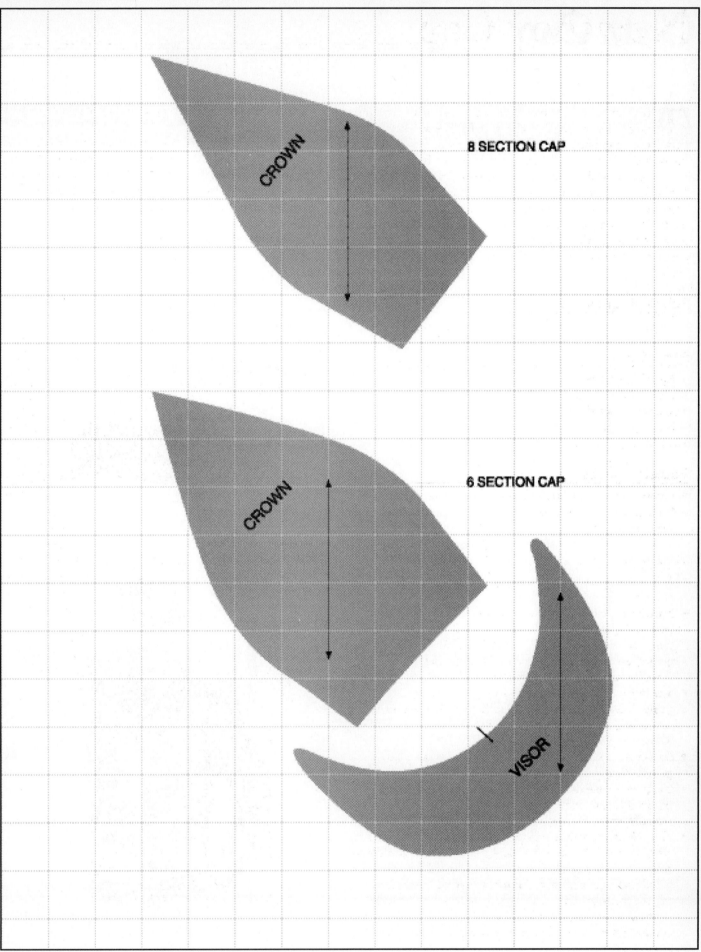

CROWN

8 SECTION CAP

CROWN

6 SECTION CAP

VISOR

Pattern is 50% actual size.

Golf Cap

A Golf cap is a man's sport cap with round flat top, fitted headband and visor. It is named for the sport for which it is most frequently worn. At the present time, this is also often referred to as a driving cap. When the brim and the crown are snapped together this is also called a snap-brim cap. This pattern is appropriate for the two husband characters in *Fallen Angels* by Noel Coward, who go off to play a game of golf in Act One, or for the picnic scene in the musical *The Pajama Game*.

Fabric Suggestions

- Seersucker, corduroy, lightweight wool, novelty cottons

Materials

- ½ yard fabric
- ½ yard lining
- Visor board, cardboard or double buckram
- ⅔ yard grosgrain ribbon #5 or ⅞" petersham

Pattern Pieces

- Side (cut 2 fabric and 2 lining)
- Top (cut 1 fabric and 1 lining)
- Visor (cut 2 fabric with seam allowances and 1 board without seam allowance)

Construction

- Following the instructions on page 3, enlarge pattern pieces and cut.
- *Crown:* With right sides together, stitch center front seams of the side. Press seam open and topstitch on both sides of seam.
- Fold top piece in half, right sides together, and stitch the dart. Clip the seam allowance at the top of the dart to the stitch line—this will allow you to press the seam open. Topstitch.
- With right sides together, match the center front seam of the side pieces to the center front notch of the top piece. Pin from the center out in each direction, easing curves as you go. Stitch seam and clip curves. Press seam allowance toward side and topstitch.
- Repeat this construction with the lining pieces.
- Place lining inside cap, right sides out, matching the center front seam, side back seams and center back dart. Stitch together.
- *Visor:* With right sides together, stitch around front edge of visor cover pieces. Clip curves and turn. Slip visor board into cover fabric, putting all seam allowances toward one side of board, which will become the bottom side of visor. Smoothing the fabric gently towards opening, pin seam allowances together and baste close to visor. Topstitch ½ inch in from outside curved edge. With right sides together, match center front of cap with centerline of visor. Pin out from center. Stitch visor to cap.
- Cut a piece of grosgrain ribbon or petersham to fit the actor's head plus seam allowances. Fold back one seam allowance. Pin ribbon to bottom edge seam allowance, matching top edge of ribbon to inner edge of seam allowance. Hand or machine stitch. (It is difficult to machine stitch the ribbon to the cap where the visor is attached.)
- Fold ribbon up into cap, covering all raw edges. Tack the visor to the center front seam of cap or sew on a small snap.

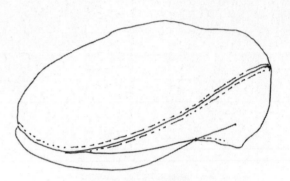

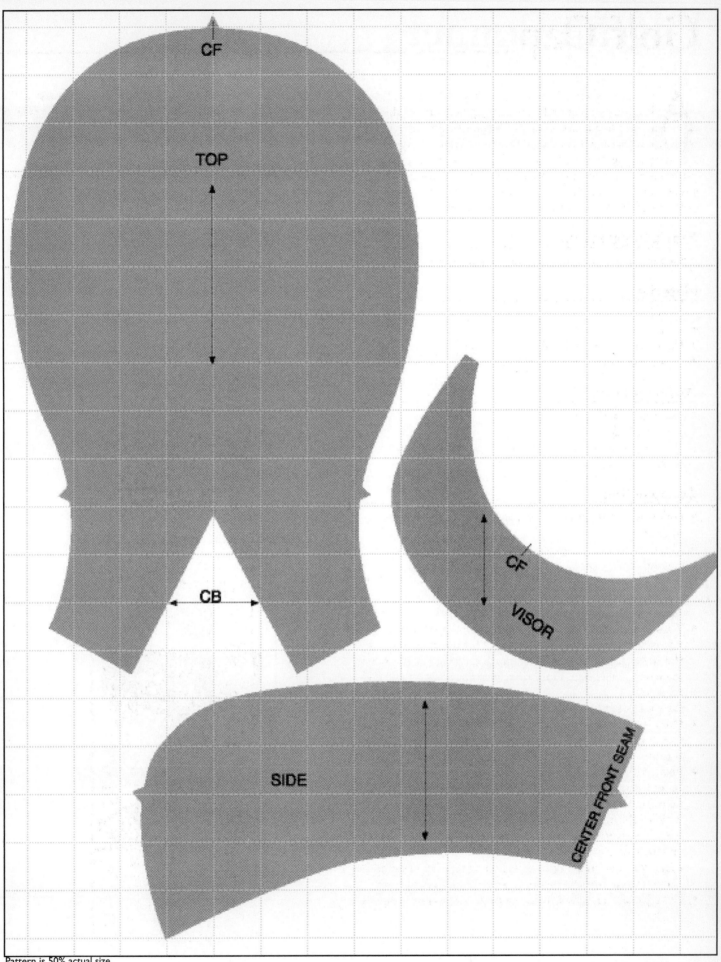

CF

TOP

CB

VISOR

CF

SIDE

CENTER FRONT SEAM

Pattern is 50% actual size.

Pilgrim Bonnet

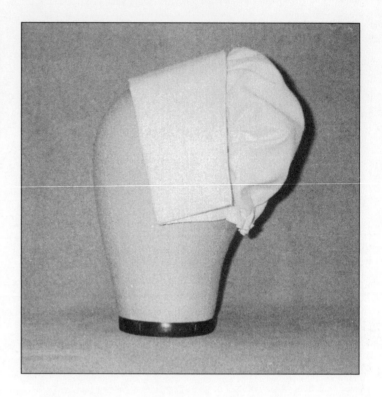

This small cloth cap was worn by Pilgrim women and girls. This style of cap also continued through later periods, worn by female servants. With an extension of the brim, it is the basis of many styles of bonnets worn through the beginning of the 20th century. This bonnet would be used in productions of *The Crucible*, or for a Thanksgiving pageant.

Fabric Suggestions

- Stiff white cotton, linen

Materials

- ½ yard fabric
- ¼ yard of ¾ inch elastic
- ⅓ yard 1-inch single-fold bias tape
- Ties, optional
- 1 yard edging, optional

Pattern Pieces

- Brim (cut 2)
- Bonnet back (cut 1)

Construction

- Following the instructions on page 3, enlarge pattern pieces and cut.
- *Brim:* With right sides together, stitch around the outside edges of three sides of brim, leaving crown edge open. Clip curves and corners. Turn right side out. Press and topstitch or trim outside edges. Baste across the open edge of the brim within the seam allowance.
- *Bonnet Back:* Cut a 12" piece of bias tape and open bottom fold. Lay bias tape face down along bottom edge of bonnet back, aligning edge with opened edge of tape. Stitch on fold line of tape. Press seam allowance toward tape and topstitch through tape and the seam allowance, being sure not to sew through bonnet. Sew top edge of tape to bonnet, forming a casing. Insert elastic into casing and sew to seam allowances at both ends.
- Sew a gathering stitch along curved edges of bonnet back as indicated. Gather to fit brim.
- With right sides together, pin bonnet back to front brim, matching center front points. Stitch. Finish raw edges of seam allowance.
- Attach ties and trim as desired.

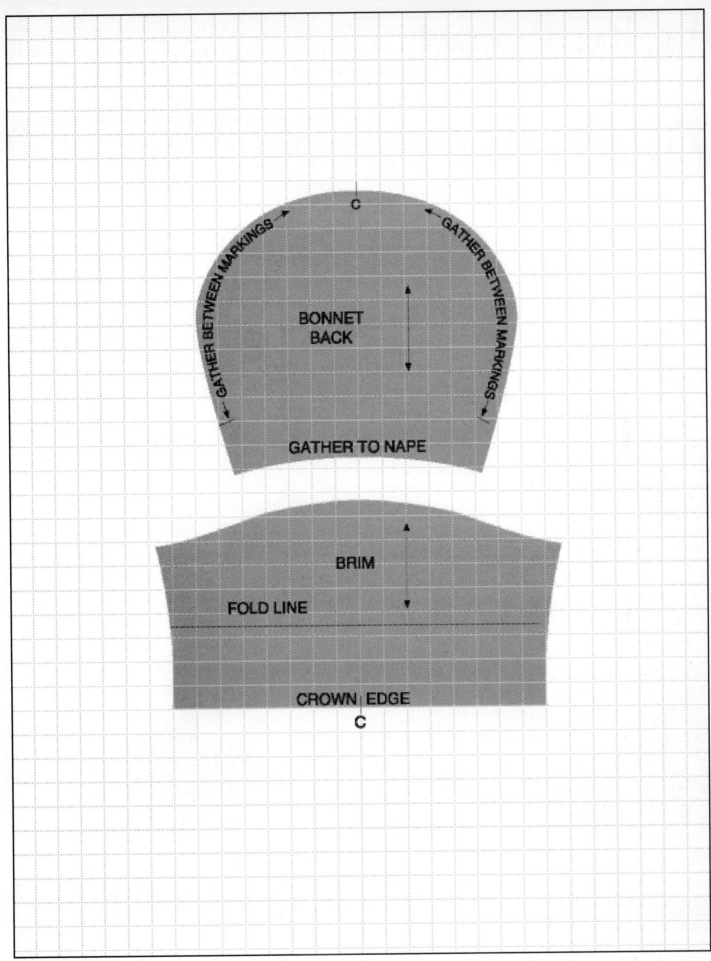

GATHER BETWEEN MARKINGS

GATHER BETWEEN MARKINGS

C

BONNET
BACK

GATHER TO NAPE

BRIM

FOLD LINE

CROWN EDGE

C

Pattern is 25% actual size.

Prairie Bonnet

A prairie bonnet is a cloth or straw hat with a projecting brim at the front. It is tied under the chin and worn by women and children. Prairie bonnets gained popularity during the 1800s, especially in the western or "untamed" portion of the United States. It is still worn today by members of the Amish Faith. This pattern would be perfect for a production of *Oklahoma!*, *Seven Brides for Seven Bothers*, or *Paint Your Wagon*.

Fabric Suggestions

- Sturdy cotton or linen, gingham, calico, huck-toweling

Materials

- ½ yard fabric
- ¼ yard of ¾-inch elastic
- ½ yard 1-inch single fold bias tape
- Ties of ribbon or, more usually, self fabric, optional
- 1 yard edging, optional
- ¼ yard interfacing (if the brim needs stiffening)
- 20 inches of 2-inch bias of face fabric or 1-inch double fold bias tape

Pattern Pieces

- Brim (cut 2 fabric, 1 interfacing if needed to stiffen the brim)
- Bonnet back (cut 1)
- Self-fabric ties (cut 2)

Construction

- Following the instructions on page 3, enlarge pattern pieces and cut. If the fabric chosen needs more body, flat line with interfacing on the wrong side of one of the brim pieces.
- *Brim:* With right sides together, stitch around the outer three sides of brim leaving notched edge open. Clip curves and corners, turn right sides out and press. Topstitch or trim outside edges of brim. Baste across the open edge of brim within seam allowances.
- *Bonnet Back:* Place bias tape on bonnet back as indicated to create a casing. Stitch in place. On either side of the bonnet back piece, below the casing, double fold and hem the two sides of what will become the neck ruffle. Hem bottom edge of bonnet back. Insert elastic into the casing and stitch to seam allowances at both ends.
- Sew a gathering stitch along the bonnet back from casing edge to casing edge. Gather.
- With right sides together, pin bonnet back to front brim match-ing the center front points and the side points as indicated (A to A and B to B). Stitch.
- *Self-fabric ties:* Fold each of the tie pieces in half the long way with right sides together. Stitch down the long side and the an-gled end. Clip corners and turn right side out. Repeat with the second tie. Press. Pin ties to inside of brim as indicated and stitch in place.
- Bind raw edge of hat where the brim and the crown join with a strip of bias fabric or bias tape and encase raw edges of seam and ties.

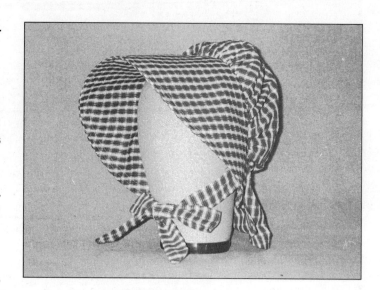

17359—Sunbonnet of Blue and White Checked Gingham, or Blue Figured Percale. No size required in ordering. State ma-terial desired......*OUR PRICE,* **Two for .49; each .25** —*we pay postage and expressage.*

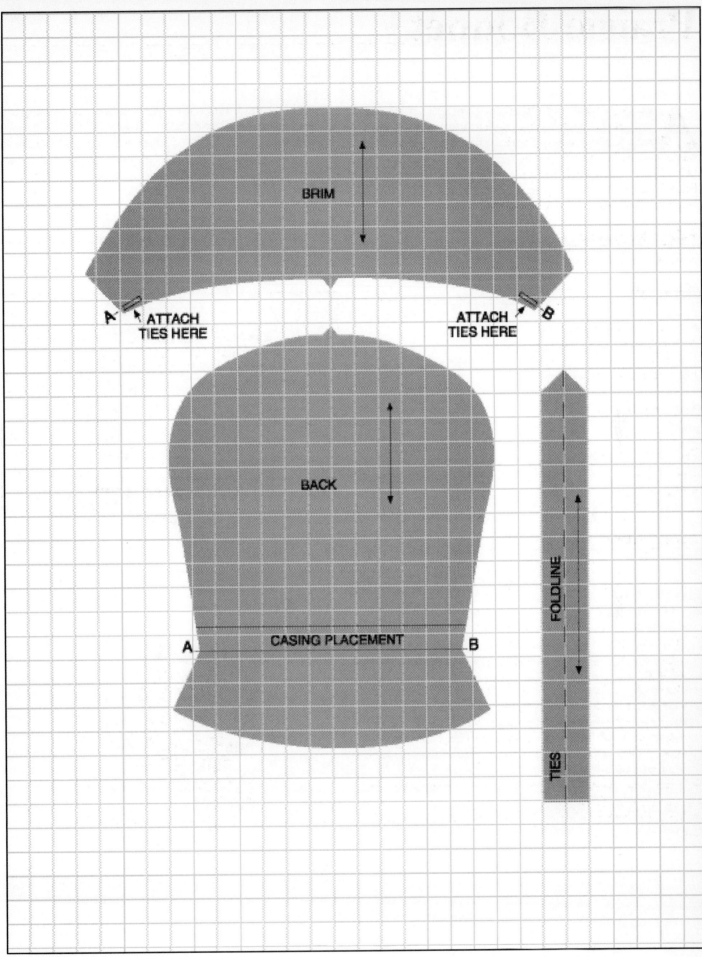

BRIM

ATTACH
TIES HERE

A

ATTACH
TIES HERE

B

BACK

A

CASING PLACEMENT

B

FOLDLINE

TIES

Pattern is 25% actual size.

Woman's Snood

A Snood is a small mesh cap worn to conceal or confine the wearer's hair. This simple snood pattern works well for the fashions of the mid 1800's and 1940's. This pattern is perfect for women in Civil War era reenactments or the productions of *Little Women*, *Oliver*, *A Christmas Carol*, and many of the plays set in the 1940's like *The Women* or *The Man Who Came To Dinner*.

Suggested Fabrics

- Various nets, loose knits, crocheted laces

Materials

- ½ yard fabric
- 13 inches of ¼" elastic
- ⅓ yard ½" single fold bias tape
- Horsehair (optional)
- Ribbon

Pattern Pieces

- Snood body (cut 1)

Construction

- Following the instructions on page 3, enlarge pattern piece and cut. If trimming the body of the snood, it is best to do this while the snood is flat. Sew on trims evenly spaced so that when the snood is gathered they will not appear crooked.
- Sew a bias binding/casing around the large curve (bottom edge) of the snood. Insert elastic into the casing. Pull up the elastic so it will fit snuggly from ear to ear around base of the neck, roughly 13 inches. Stitch ends of elastic into place.
- Add an easing stitch across upper curve. Pull the threads of this stitch to gather/ease curve to measure the distance from ear to ear across the top of the head (roughly 10 inches). Stitch binding to this edge, making sure the gathers are spread evenly.
- Stitch horsehair along the top curve for pinning snood into actor's hair or wig.
- Add decorative trim or ribbon along top edge if desired.

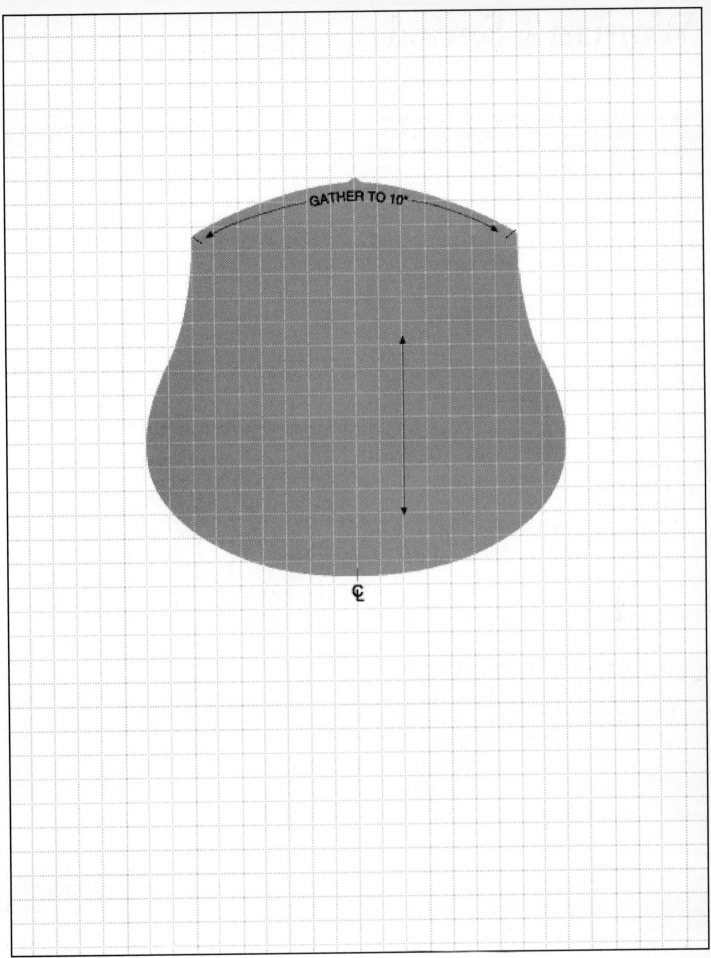

GATHER TO 10"

CL

Pattern is 25% actual size.

Spanish Man's Snood

This style of snood is typical for an 18th century Spanish man and is found in many paintings of Francisco Goya. This would be worn in productions of *The Marriage of Figaro*, *The Barber of Seville*, or *Don Giovanni*.

Fabric Suggestions

- Netting, lace, fishnet, loose weave knit

Materials

- ⅝ yard fabric
- ⅝ yard lining (optional)
- Decorative trims as desired
- ⅔ yard ½" single fold bias tape
- Tassel 4" - 6" long

Pattern Pieces

- Snood body (cut 1)

Construction

- Following the instructions on page 3, enlarge pattern piece and cut.
- If trimming the body of the snood, it is best to do this while the snood is flat, being sure that when the seams are put together the trims will flow as desired.
- Flat line before or after decorating if the face fabric needs the stability of the lining, or use the lining to "clean-up" the inside of the snood.
- With right sides together, stitch up the back seam. Press seam open. Gather the bottom edge and stitch together. Turn right side out.
- Hand stitch tassel to the gathered point.
- Stitch a basting stitch along the top curve of the snood from notch to notch, as indicated on pattern. Gather the stitch to fit actor's head and bind the edge. You may want to sew horsehair along the top edge for pinning snood to actor's hair or wig.
- Add trim along top edge if desired.

Snoods for *La Traviata*, designed by Desmond Heeley.

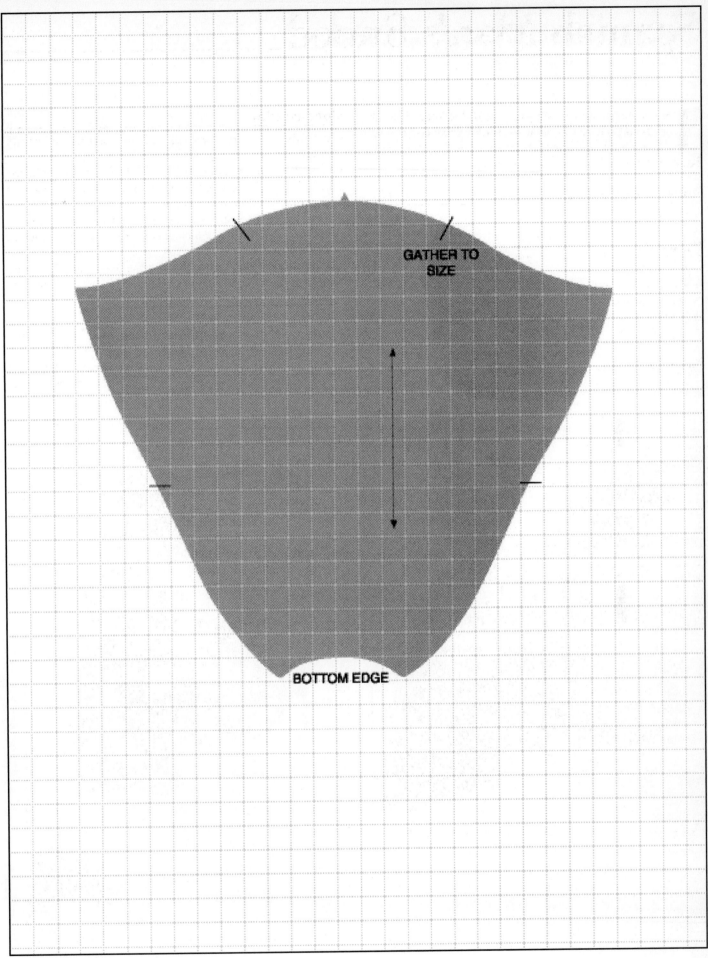

GATHER TO SIZE

BOTTOM EDGE

Pattern is 25% actual size.

Renaissance Snood

This pattern is for a fuller snood, popular during the Renaissance. For most theatrical purposes, it will not be filled with hair and should be opaque when lined. A version of this snood was made for the revival of *Kiss Me Kate* on Broadway, designed by Martin Pakledinaz. You will find this snood very useful in many of the Shakespeare plays and a large number of operas.

Fabric Suggestions

- Rich brocade, lace, fancy net, novelty knit

Materials

- ¾ yard face fabric
- ¾ yard lining (optional)
- ⅔ yard ½" single fold bias tape
- Horsehair
- Trims as desired

Pattern Pieces

- Snood body (cut 1)
- Neck inset piece (cut 1)

Construction

- Following the instructions on page 3, enlarge pattern pieces and cut.
- If trimming the body of the snood, it is best to do this while the snood is flat.
- Stitch a double row of gathering stitches around the outside of large curve. Keep ends free to pull up later.
- With right sides together, pin center of snood bottom edge to the center back of neck inset, matching A notches. Pin end corner of snood to corners of neck inset, matching B points.
- Pull gathering threads to fit snood body to neck inset. Pin, making sure the gathering is even. Stitch. Press seam allowance toward neck inset piece. Topstitch in place through all layers.
- Pin small tucks or gather at the top edge between notches as indicated. Stitch in place.
- Stitch bias tape around head opening. Stitch horsehair along top for pinning to actor's hair or wig.
- Add trims to front edge as desired.

Snood for *Rigoletto*, designed by Carl Thoms.

Snood for *Kiss Me Kate*, designed by Martin Pakledinaz.

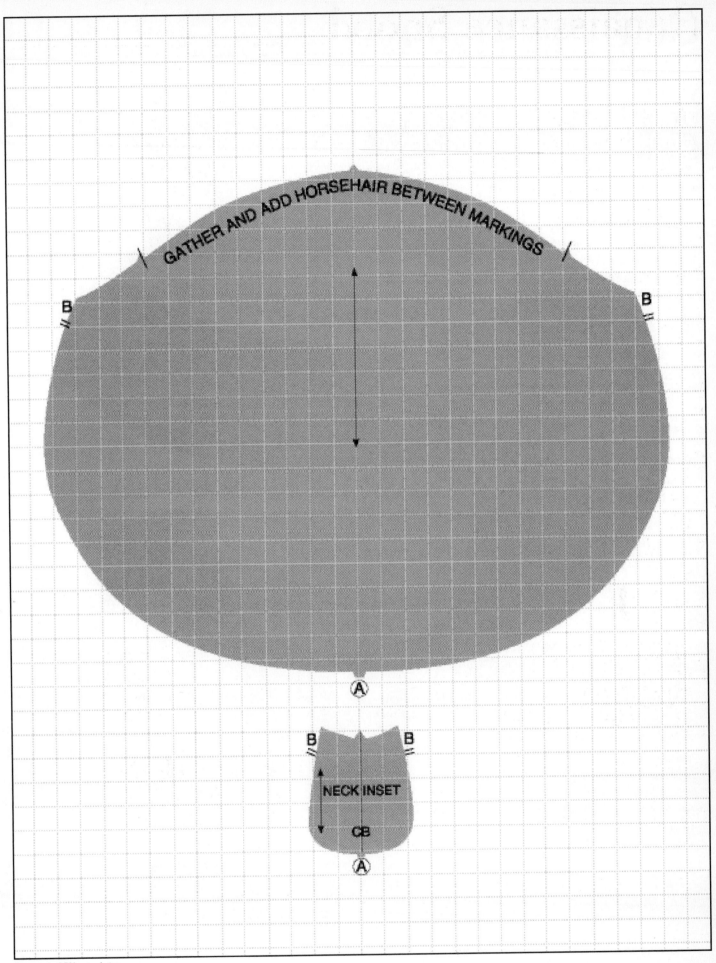

GATHER AND ADD HORSEHAIR BETWEEN MARKINGS

B

B

Ⓐ

B NECK INSET B

CB

Ⓐ

Pattern is 25% actual size.

Coif

A coif is a simple fitted head covering similar in shape to a baby's bonnet. The coif popular during the Middle Ages had extended sides and was tied under the chin. Coifs were also worn in the 17th and 18th century by the working classes. In Commedia dell'arte, Pantalone is usually wearing a coif. Coifs are also worn by old peasants in many plays taking place during Medieval times or the Renaissance. This pattern is also good as a base for other draped headpieces such as wimples and turbans.

We have included two different side piece patterns. One points toward the front to tie under the chin, the other curves in front of the ear. A coif made with the curved front works well as a head covering base for soft draped hats such as turbans.

Fabric Suggestions

- Linen, noile, osnaburg, monk's cloth, thin wool

Materials

- ½ yard face fabric
- ½ yard lining, if bag lining the hat
- Cording or ribbon for ties

Pattern Pieces

- Side piece (cut 2 fabric and 2 lining [optional] for style variation desired)
- Center piece (cut 2 fabric and 2 lining [optional])

Construction

- Following the instructions on page 3, enlarge pattern pieces and cut.
- With right sides together, stitch center pieces together along notched edge.
- With right sides together, stitch one side piece to each side of the center pieces, matching marks (It is easier if the center piece is on the bottom when sewing.). Clip seam allowance around curves and press open. Topstitch if desired.
- Bind the edges of the coif or make a second coif of lining fabric. With right sides together, pin the lining to the coif. Stitch around the sides leaving a space open at back of neck. Clip curves and corners and turn right side out. Press edges. Hand sew the opening closed.
- Add ties if desired.

Note: if you are using the coif as an inner structure not to be seen, press seam allowances toward the center and topstitch—this makes the seams sturdier.

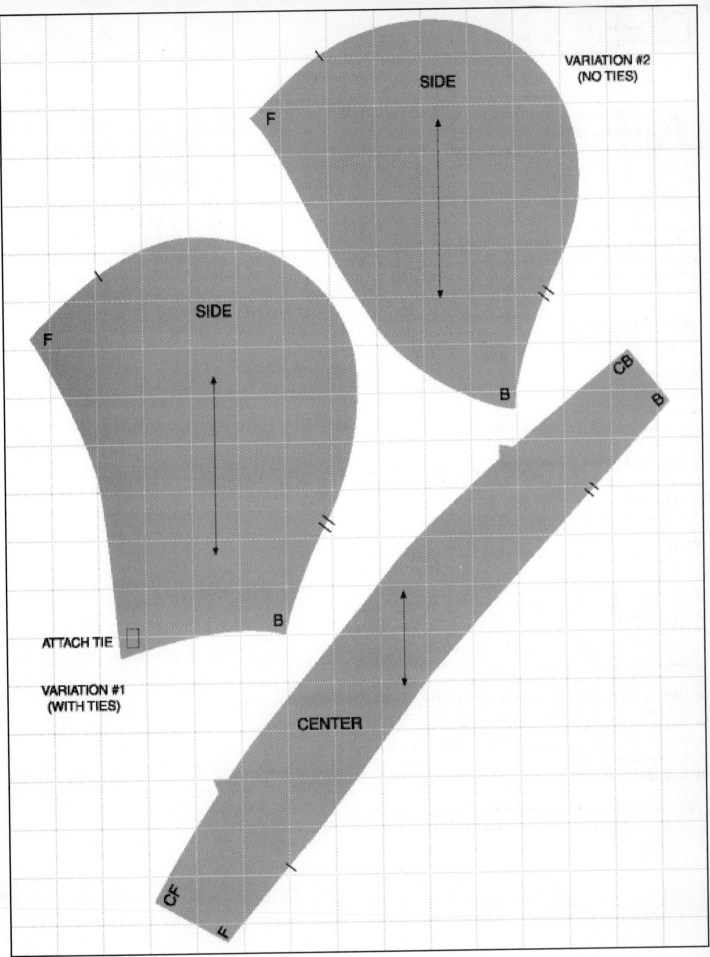

VARIATION #2
(NO TIES)

SIDE

F

B

SIDE

F

CB

B

ATTACH TIE

VARIATION #1
(WITH TIES)

CENTER

CF

F

Pattern is 50% actual size.

Nurse's Cap

The white heavily starched cap that we think of as a nurse's cap dates to the beginning of the 20th century. Prior to this time, nurses wore a variation of a nun's habit (logical since many of the hospitals were staffed by the nuns), a headscarf, or a type of mob cap. As hairstyles became smaller, so did the cap. In the early 20th century, individual nursing schools began to pick a specific style of cap to represent them. You could tell a nurse's alma mater by looking at her cap. There are literally hundreds of styles of nurse's caps. We have chosen two basic styles that you can alter as desired. Historically, senior student nurses added a 1/4-inch black band to their caps. A graduate replaced this with a 1/2-inch band. The ribbon is usually pinned on so it can be removed when washing the cap.

Fabric Suggestions

- Heavy weight cotton or linen

Materials

- ½ yard fabric
- ½ yard woven iron-on interfacing (if needed)
- 2 buttons ¼-inch wide with a shank

Pattern Pieces

- Cap (cut 2) of desired variation.

Construction

- Following the instructions on page 3, enlarge pattern piece and cut.
- If your fabric is not very stiff, you may want to add a stiff woven interfacing to the wrong side.
- With right sides together, stitch around the cap, leaving the flat edge on the back of the cap open. Clip corners, turn right sides out and press. Slipstitch the opening closed.
- At this point you may wish to fold the back flaps together and stitch closed or make buttonholes as indicated. Real nurses' caps are buttoned together so they can be washed, heavily starched and refolded.
- Sew buttons as indicated.
- Fold the front edge back along fold line.
- Fold the back flap down. Secure the buttons through the buttonholes.

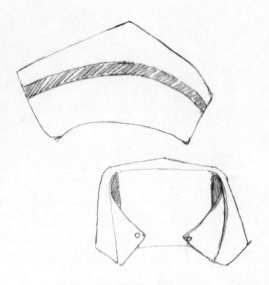

Pointed Front

Square Front

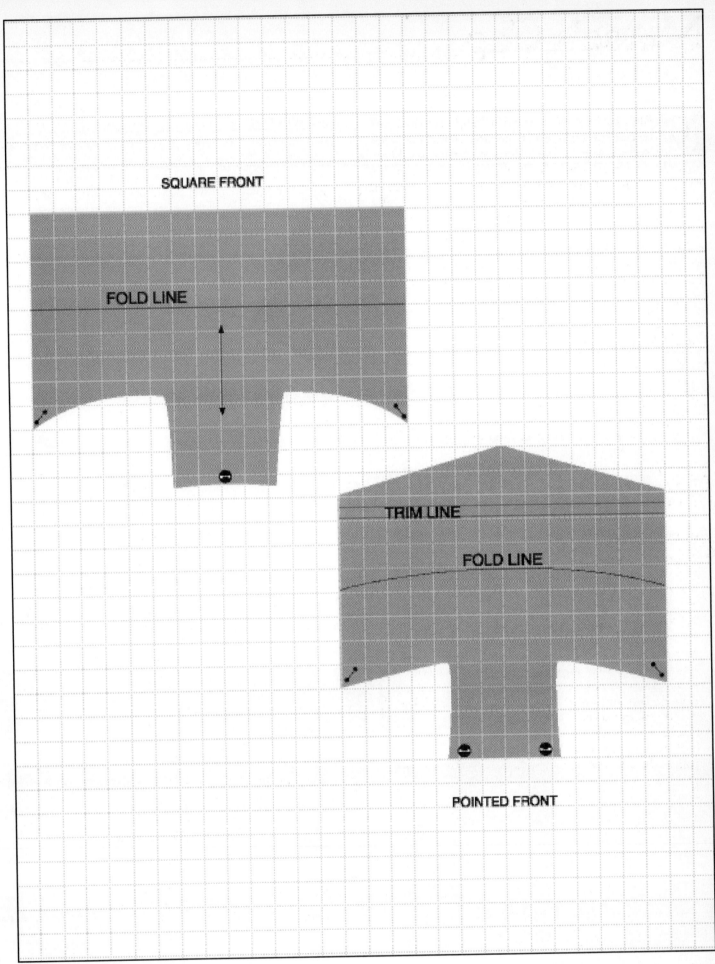

SQUARE FRONT

FOLD LINE

TRIM LINE

FOLD LINE

POINTED FRONT

Pattern is 25% actual size.

Mitre

Mitres are tall ornamented caps with points in the front and back, worn by popes, bishops, and abbots as a sign of rank. They are sometimes worn with a cardinal's cap/beanie or replaced by the beanie when taken off. (See Beanie pattern in this chapter.) This hat might find its way into productions of *Murder in the Cathedral*, *Becket*, or *The Devils*.

Fabric Suggestions

- Ecclesiastic brocades, satin, damask, faille

Materials

- ½ yard face fabric
- ½ yard lining fabric
- Ribbon or fabric for lappets
- Gold or silver metallic, or brocade ribbon trim, optional
- Buckram, cap mesh or flexible board
- Spray adhesive or Wonder-Under

Pattern Pieces

- Mitre front (cut 1 fabric, 1 inner structure [without seam allowance], and 1 lining)
- Mitre back (cut 1 fabric, 1 inner structure [without seam allowance], and 1 lining)
- Lappets (cut 2 fabric and 2 lining)

Construction

- Following the instructions on page 3, enlarge pattern pieces and cut.
- Attach face fabric, with seam allowances, to front of base shape board with spray adhesive, glue or Wonder-Under. Turn seam allowance over edge of base shape and attach to back side.
- Attach trims to front of mitre as desired.
- With right sides together, stitch lappets to linings around both sides and bottom of piece, clip corners and turn. (You may choose to use a length of decorative ribbon instead.) Place one lappet on either side of center back line on back piece of mitre. Stitch in place.
- Press back seam allowances of lining pieces to wrong side of fabric. Place lining on wrong side of base pieces, pin in place and stitch.
- Hand stitch front and back together at side seams, or with right sides out stitch fronts to back pieces close to edges.
- Glue or tack trims as desired.

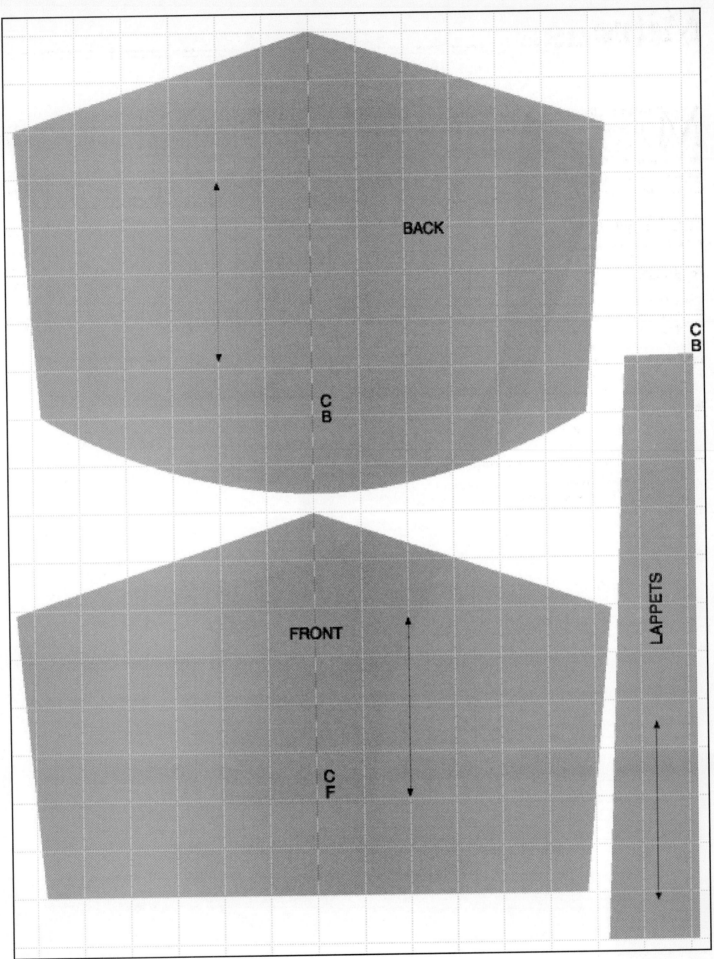

BACK

C
B

C
B

LAPPETS

FRONT

C
F

Pattern is 50% actual size.

Crows

W̲e have included a couple of basic crown shapes to use as a guide. Depending on the final desired effect, you may simply cut them out and decorate them.

Material Suggestions

- Metal sheeting, plastic, buckram

Cover Materials

- ⅓-yard fabric—lame, brocade, foil
- Assorted trims and jewels as desired

Pattern Pieces

- Crown (cut 1)

Construction

- Following the instructions on page 3, enlarge pattern pieces and cut.
- Cover or decorate as desired. If you are cutting the crown out of metal, be sure to sand all edges well.

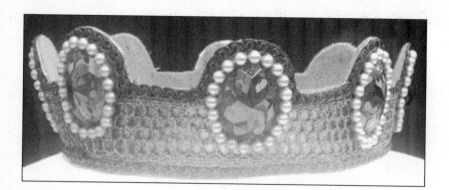

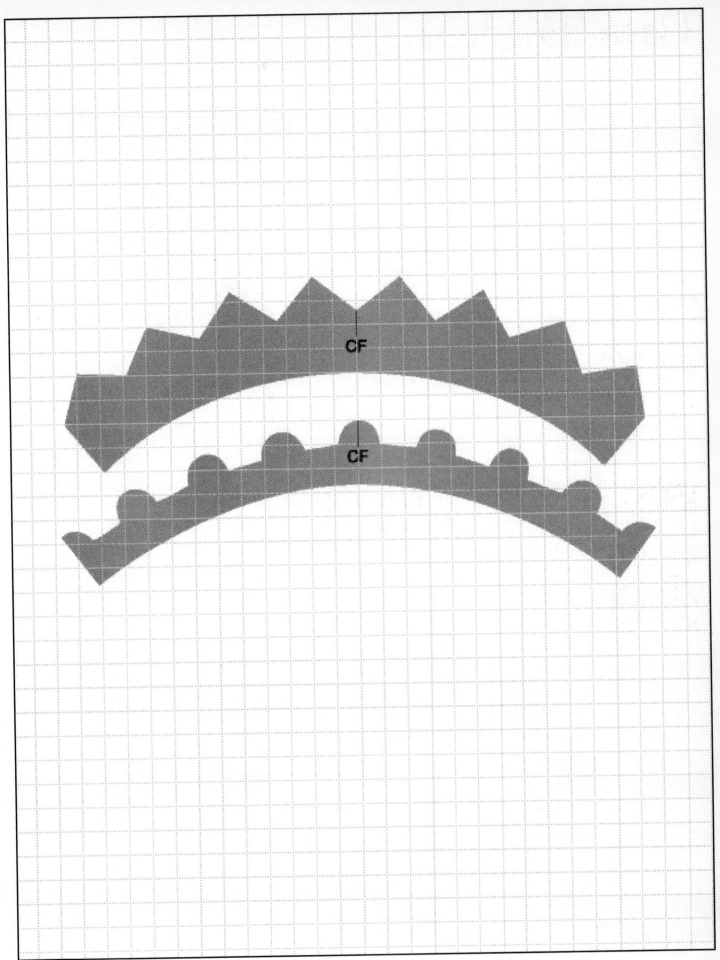

CF

CF

Pattern is 25% actual size.

Tiara/Diadem

A Tiara or Diadem is a small crown-like ornament. This basic shape can be used for many periods from ancient Greek and Roman through Renaissance, Napoleonic and into fantasy worlds.

Fabric Suggestions

- Lame, brocade

Materials

- ¼ yard stiff interfacing: buckram, thin stiff plastic or cardboard
- ¼ yard face fabric
- ¼ yard lining
- Wonder-Under or glue
- Trims as desired
- Nylon/poly horsehair or ribbon for loops

Pattern Pieces

- Diadem (cut 1 inner structure, without seam allowances; cut 2 fabric with seam allowances)

Construction

- Following the instructions on page 3, enlarge pattern pieces and cut.
- If using buckram, cut out one layer with no seam allowances. Wire edges if desired. Or cut one layer of stiff interfacing or

cardboard. Bond this piece to wrong side of face fabric with Wonder-Under or glue.
- Line back with felt or fold back seam allowance toward diadem and stitch in place.
- Trim as desired.
- Attach horsehair along the bottom edge or add small loops for pinning to acto'rs wig or hair.

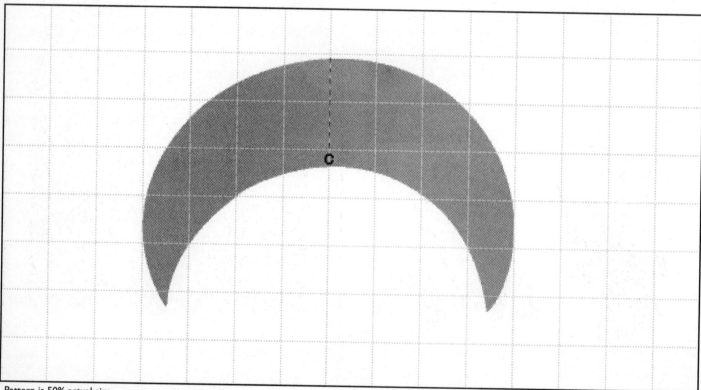

Pattern is 50% actual size.

Bag for Bag Wig

This bag is tied around the ponytail of a man's wig or Peruke. This style of wig was popular in the mid 1700's and would be perfect for a production of *Dangerous Liaisons*, *She Stoops To Conquer*, *Our Country's Good* or *1776*.

Fabric Suggestions

- Satin, faille or taffeta (usually black)

Materials

- ¼ yard fabric
- ¼-inch wide ties or grosgrain ribbon #1½
- Ribbon for bow

Pattern Pieces

- Bag (cut 1)

Construction

- Following the instructions on page 3, enlarge pattern piece and cut.
- With right sides together, fold rectangle in half crosswise. Sew the 2 sides from the fold to 1 inch short of the end.
- Double fold the top edge of the bag. Stitch in ⅜ inch from the edge to form a casing. Thread ribbon or tie through the casing, with a portion coming out at each seam.
- Stitch the tie to the seam of the bag on what will be the underside, so that the ties will not pull out during use.
- Make a larger bow of grosgrain or satin ribbon and stitch to the front of the top casing. Almost any style or size bow may be used, depending on the character being portrayed. Historically, these bows were anywhere from narrow strings, sometimes multi-looped, to pieces almost as wide as the actor's shoulders.

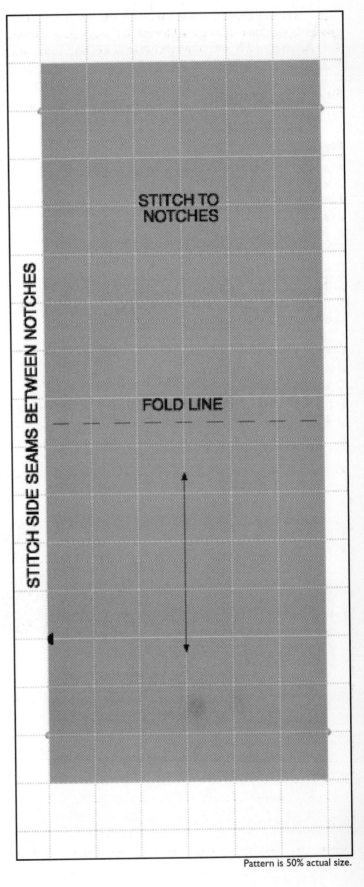

STITCH TO NOTCHES

STITCH SIDE SEAMS BETWEEN NOTCHES

FOLD LINE

Pattern is 50% actual size.

Chaperone

This ancient hood covering for head and shoulders was worn by men and women in Middle Ages through the Renaissance. In a simple form, this pattern can be used for a monk's hood and cowl and is a great accessory for productions of *Robin Hood* or for a renaissance faire. You might also find it useful in many of the Shakespeare plays.

Fabric Suggestions

• Medium weight velvet, linen, drapery fabric, or wool

Materials

• 1½ yards fabric
• 1½ yard lining

Pattern Pieces

• Chaperone (cut 2 fabric and 2 lining)

Note: If you want a dagged or castellated edge along the shoulder, mark the appropriate edging on the wrong side of the face fabric before you begin putting the pieces together.

Construction

• Following the instructions on page 3, enlarge pattern piece and cut.
• If piece was not cut on the fold, sew top seam of both the fabric and the lining.
• With right sides together, stitch back seam, clip curves and press.
• With right sides together, stitch center front seam, clip curves and press.
• Repeat above steps with the lining.
• With right sides together, stitch lining to fabric at shoulder edge. If you want a castellated or dagged edge, sew along this shaped line. Clip curves and corners, turn fabric right sides out and press. Topstitch if desired.
• With lining up in chaperone, turn seam allowances of fabric and lining around the face opening to the inside and slipstitch closed.
• If the hood is always being worn back off of the head, you may want to tack it into a pleasant arrangement.

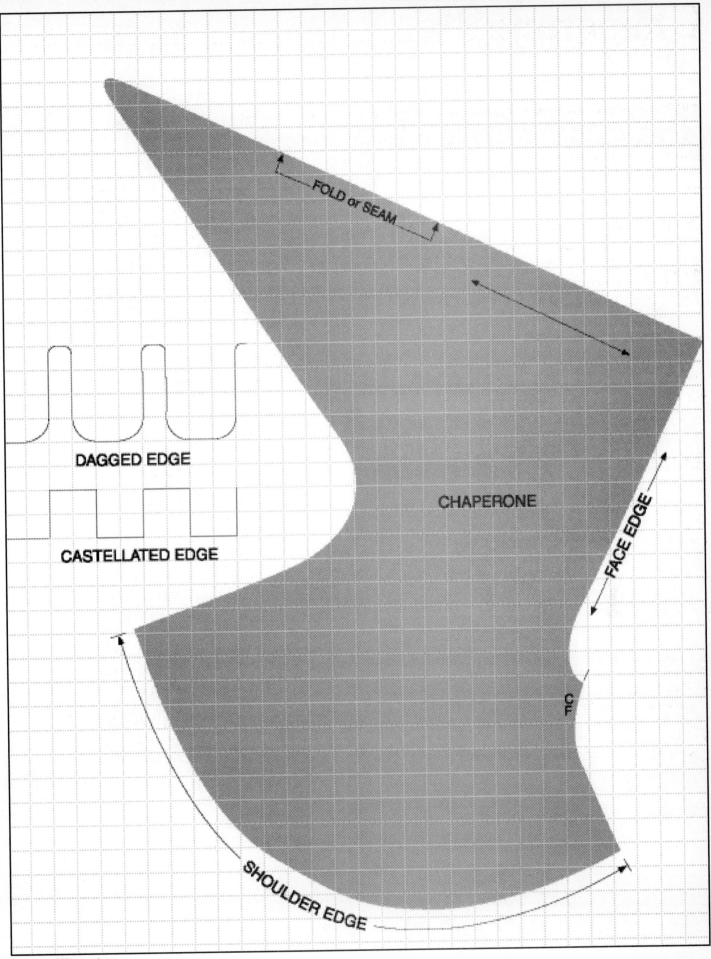

FOLD or SEAM

DAGGED EDGE

CASTELLATED EDGE

CHAPERONE

FACE EDGE

CF

SHOULDER EDGE

Pattern is 25% actual size.

Chapter 2

NECKWEAR

Cravat

A cravat is a long scarf of fabric or lace tied around the neck in a variety of styles. Earlier cravats came from the back of the neck and either tied or knotted in front. Sometimes they were tied together with a separate ribbon called a ribband.

A Dickensian cravat is longer than others and has finished ends. To tie, begin with the center of the cravat at the neck front (under the chin). Bring each end around the neck, cross ends in back, bring back around front, and tie in a knot or a bow.

A Steinkirk is a long cravat often with lace or fringe edges tied and worn with one end tucked through a buttonhole or pinned to the coat front or to the waistcoat. Women also wore this style of cravat tucked into a buttonhole or corset lacing. This style was fashionable for the last third of the 17th century and well into the 18th century.

Dickensian Cravat

- Finished size is 60 inches by 4 inches

Fabric Suggestions

- Taffeta, doupioni silk, lightweight brocades

Construction

- Cut a length of fabric 61 inches by 9 inches.
- Fold in half lengthwise, right sides together, and stitch along the 3 open sides using a ½ inch seam allowance. Keep 5 inches at the center of the long side open, in order to turn the cravat right side out. Clip corners, turn right sides out and press. Slip-stitch opening closed.

Steinkirk

- Finished size is 52 inches by 5 inches.

Fabric Suggestions

- Soft cotton shirtings

Construction

- Cut a length of fabric 53 inches by 6 inches.
- Hem all four sides with a double fold hem.
- Add lace or fringe to short ends as desired.

Cravat.

Steinkirk.

Ascot

This neck scarf or tie has broad ends and is tied so that one end falls over the other. Supposedly developed to wear at the Ascot Horse Races in England, this is the type of neck scarf that gets tucked into the neck of a dressing gown or 1970s casual wear. This neck accessory seems to find its way into almost every play by Noel Coward.

Fabric Suggestions

• Silk, polyester, brocades, tie fabrics

Materials

• 1 yard fabric

Pattern Pieces

• Ascot (cut 2)

Construction

• Following the instructions on page 3, enlarge pattern pieces and cut.
• With right sides together, sew around the body of the ascot, leaving a space center back through which to turn the ascot right-side out. Clip corners. Turn right-side out and press. Hand stitch the opening closed.
• Pleat the back as indicated on the pattern. Pin through all layers and stitch.
• Press the pleats to one side and stitch down flat.

Costume design by Arnold S. Levine for Simon in *Hayfever*.

JOIN PATTERN PIECES BEFORE CUTTING

JOIN PATTERN PIECES BEFORE CUTTING

Pattern is 25% actual size.

Formalwear Ascot _____

This is a modern variation of a true ascot. In a 1920s Sears & Roebuck catalog it was called a puff scarf or a puff tie. In the 20th century it is usually worn with strollers and mourning suits. You can use this style in your production of *My Fair Lady*, or any play with a daytime formal wedding, such as *The Philadelphia Story*. For a 19th century style, make the front piece wider and the joiner longer.

Fabric Suggestions

* Medium weight silk, tie silks, polyester, damask, soft brocades

Materials

* ⅜ yard fabric
* Velcro or hook and bar
* Decorative button or jewel

Pattern Pieces

* Neckband (cut 1)
* Front (cut 1)
* Joiner (cut 1)

Construction

* Following the instructions on page 3, enlarge pattern pieces and cut. If you want the ascot to have diagonal stripes, cut the front on the bias. There is no structural reason for the bias cut.

Neck Band

* Fold the neckband lengthwise, right sides together. Stitch, turn and press.

Front Piece

* Machine hem short ends of front. Fold front in half lengthwise and stitch. Press seam open. Turn the resulting tube right side with seam down center of the underside. Press. Pleat center of front as indicated on pattern.

Joiner

* With right sides together, stitch around joiner leaving the short straight edge open for turning. Clip corners, turn and press flat. Stitch the opening closed. Fold the joiner along fold line with folded end on top—this will be the back side of the finished ascot.
* Lay pleated front on joiner with pleats aligned with fold.
* Lay neckband on top of front.
* Fold joiner around front and neckband. Stitch joiner to itself so that it will slide on the neckband.
* Turn ascot over. Fold front down and cross lower edges over joiner. Pin through all layers. Stitch, adding decorative button or jewel.
* Add Velcro or skirt hook and bar to ends of neckband.

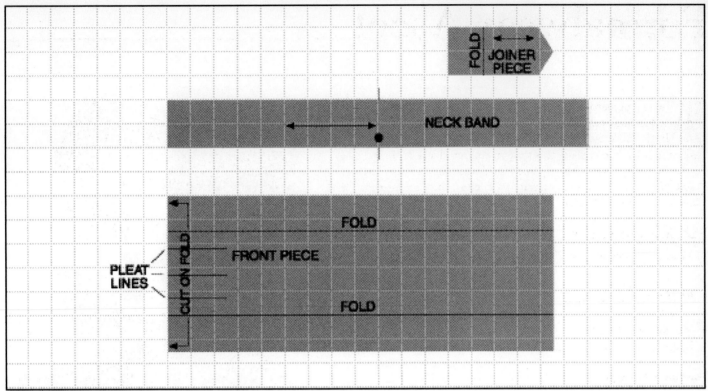

Pattern is 25% actual size.

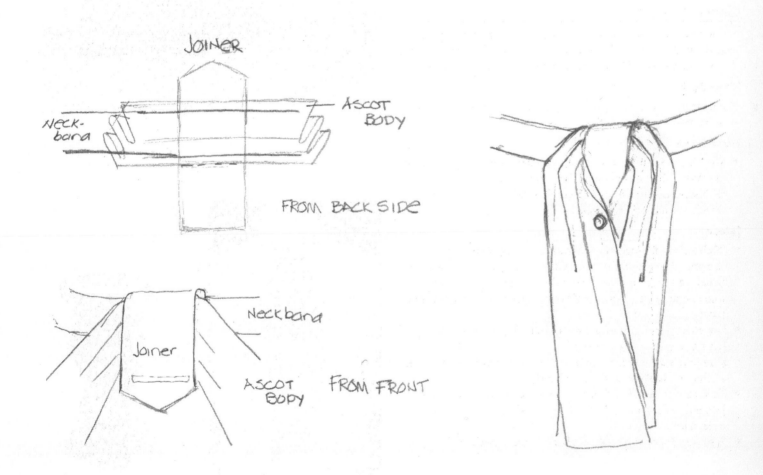

Jabot

A jabot is a fall of lace or other cloth attached to the front of a neckband and was worn especially by men in the late17th and 18th centuries. It is a necessary accessory for all Restoration comedies, especially for Moliere plays.

Fabric Suggestions

- Cotton, light weight linen, satin

Materials

- ½ yard fabric
- ½ yard pre-gathered lace or 1½ yards flat lace 3 inches wide
- Velcro, snaps, or hooks and eyes

Pattern Pieces

- Neckband (cut 1)
- Base piece (cut 2)

Construction

- Following the instructions on page 3, enlarge pattern pieces and cut.
- With right sides together, sew around the base piece leaving the top open to turn. Clip corners and curves, turn and press.
- If you are using flat lace, gather the lace by running a stitch close to top edge, or flat pleat for a more tailored look.
- Place lace at bottom edge of base, pin in place, and stitch. Place second row of lace as indicated on pattern, pin in place, and stitch. Place third row of lace at the top edge of base piece with raw edge of lace going into the seam allowance.
- Place the base piece onto the neckband as indicated, right sides together, and stitch. Press seam allowance toward the neckband.
- Press seam allowance on the opposite side toward wrong side. Press seam allowances on the back seams in as well. Press neckband in half and stitch closed.
- Add closures in back.
- Add trim to the front of the finished jabot, such as a brooch, a buckle, or a bow.

Variation

You may choose to use a narrower lace, in which case you should adjust the placement accordingly, making sure that the bottom edge of the upper row covers the stitch line of the row below. Narrower lace will require more rows.

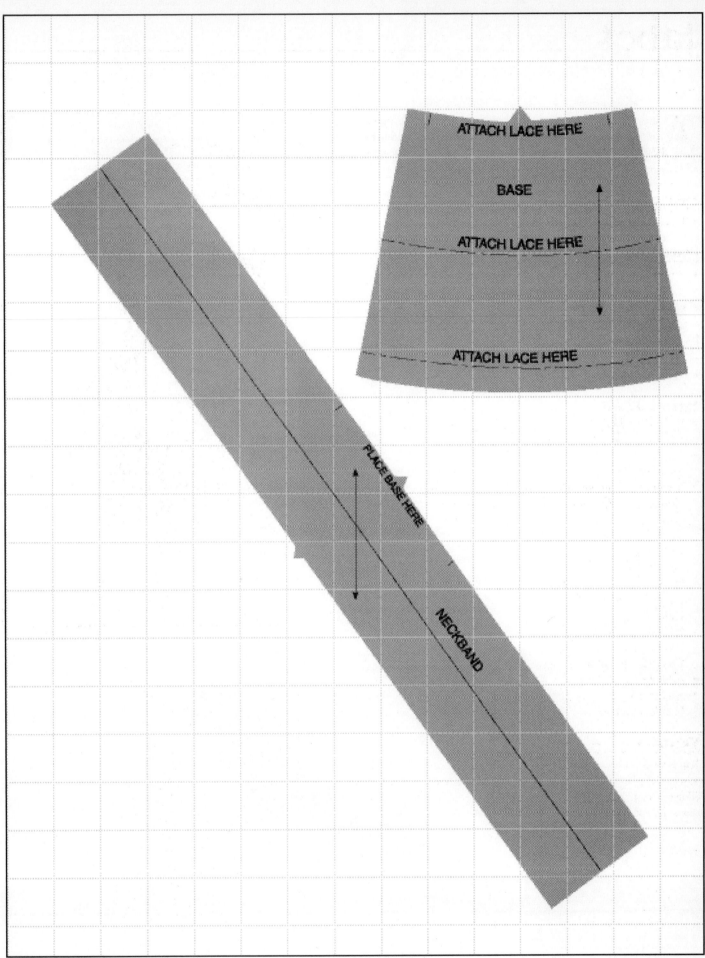

ATTACH LACE HERE

BASE

ATTACH LACE HERE

ATTACH LACE HERE

PLACE BASE HERE

NECKBAND

Pattern is 50% actual size.

Stock

This broad stiffened band is worn around the neck like a high collar and tied. Popular in the early Victorian/Dickensian period, it is perfect for *A Christmas Carol*, *Nicholas Nickleby*, or for adaptations of the works of Jane Austin. This stock fits neck sizes 14½–16 inches—adjust as necessary.

Fabric Suggestions

- Faille, silk, dupioni satin. Stocks were historically black or white. Some pastels and occasionally dark colors were worn, but stocks were rarely patterned.

Materials

- ¼ yard fabric
- ¼ yard lining
- Interfacing
- Ribbon for ties

Pattern Pieces

- Stock (cut 1 fabric, 1 lining, and 1 interfacing)

Construction

- Following the instructions on page 3, enlarge pattern piece and cut.
- Stitch interfacing to wrong side of fabric.
- Pin ties, where indicated on pattern, to right side of fabric.
- With right sides together, stitch lining to fabric, leaving a 5-inch opening at the bottom through which to turn. Be careful not to catch the ties anywhere in the seam other than the center back where pinned.
- Clip corners and curves. Turn right side out and press.
- Slipstitch opening closed.

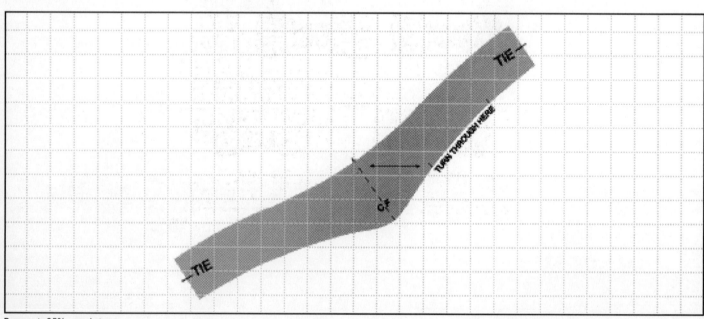

Pattern is 25% actual size.

Bow Ties

These short neckties, tied in a bow knot, were most popular at the end of the 19th and the first half of the 20th centuries. We present three styles, and the method of construction is the same for all.

These patterns fit a 15½-inch neck. If you wish to make them larger or smaller, make the adjustments at the center back.

Fabric Suggestions:

- Medium weight silks or polyesters

Materials

- ½ yard fabric
- ½ yard lightweight interfacing

Pattern Pieces

- Bow tie piece (cut 4)
- Interfacing (cut 2)

Construction

- Following the instructions on page 3, enlarge pattern pieces and cut.
- Attach interfacing to wrong side of fabric. Sew center back seams of interfaced pieces together. Sew center back seams of non-interfaced pieces. Press seams open.
- With right sides together, sew interfaced piece to non-interfaced piece. Leave an opening to turn through. Clip the curves and the corners. Turn right side out and press.
- Sew the opening closed.

Note: This makes a bow tie that must be tied for each wearing. If you want a pre-tied bow tie, extend the length of the tie pattern piece and make two half ties. Add a closure at the center back. Tie the bow and stitch into position.

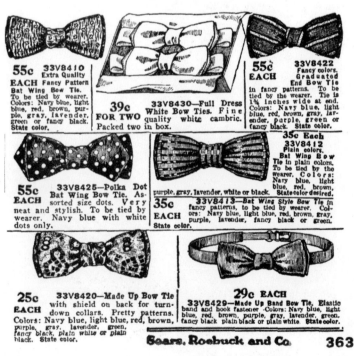

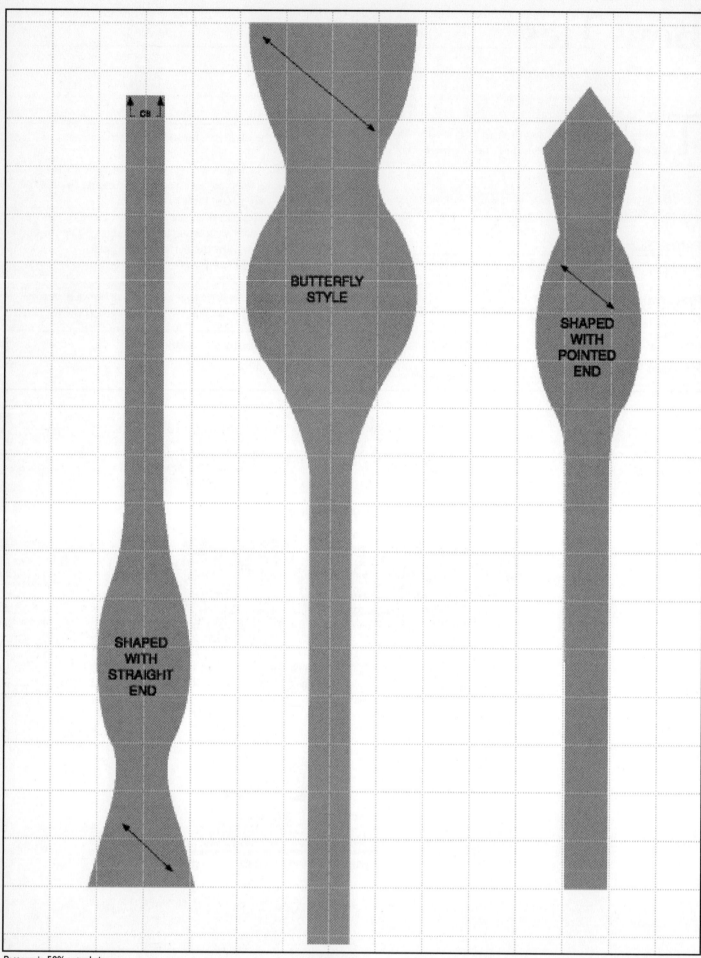

BUTTERFLY
STYLE

SHAPED
WITH
POINTED
END

CB

SHAPED
WITH
STRAIGHT
END

Pattern is 50% actual size.

How to Tie a Bow Tie

1. Start with the end in left hand, extending 1½ inches below that in the right hand.

2. Cross longer end over shorter and pass up through loop. Move knot toward neck.

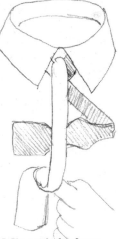

3. Form front loop of bow by doubling up shorter (hanging) end, placing across collar points.

4. Hold this front loop with thumb and forefinger of left hand. Drop long end down over front.

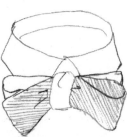

5. Place right forefinger pointing up, on bottom half of hanging part. Pass up behind front loop.

6. Poke resulting loop through knot behind front loop (as illustrated). Even ends and tighten.

How to Tie a Full Windsor (pattern and instructions follow)

1. Start with wide end of tie on your right and extending a foot below the narrow end.

2. Cross wide end over narrow and bring up through loop.

3. Bring wide end down around and behind narrow and up on your right.

4. Then put down through loop and around across narrow as shown.

5. Turn and pass up through loop. Complete by slipping down through the knot in front.

6. Tighten and draw up snug to collar.

Neckties

The familiar narrow lengths of material, worn around the neck and tied in front, neckties have changed shape throughout the years. They were extremely narrow in the 1950s and extremely wide in the 1970s. This pattern is for a tie that is 3¾" wide.

Fabric Suggestions

- Medium weight silks or polyesters. Doupioni, tie silks, medium weight jacquards.

Materials

- ½ yard fabric
- ½ yard woven interfacing like hair canvas

Pattern Pieces

- Tie front (cut 1)
- Tie back (cut 1)
- Tie midsection (cut 1)
- Front facing (cut 1)
- Back facing (cut 1)
- Front interfacing (cut 1)
- Back interfacing (cut 1)

Construction

- Following the instructions on page 3, enlarge pattern pieces and cut.
- With right sides together, stitch tie back to one end of midsection and tie front to the other end. Gently press seams open.
- Stitch front facing to tie front and stitch back facing to tie back. Clip corners and turn right side out.
- Overlap front and back interfacings and stitch through both layers—this produces a seam that is flatter than a regular seam.
- Position the interfacing down the center of the wrong side of the tie. Using a long stitch, baste into place, tucking the ends of the interfacing into the faced ends of the tie. (The interfacing will not reach to the ends of the tie.)
- Carefully and gently "finger press" the sides of the tie over the interfacing. Fold back the seam allowance of the overlapped side of the tie—the under lapped side should remain open. Loosely stitch tie closed, being sure to stitch into the interfacing but not the face fabric.

How to Tie a Half Windsor

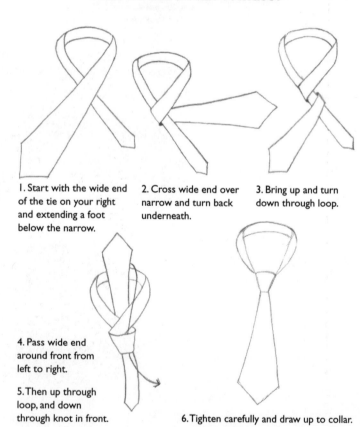

1. Start with the wide end of the tie on your right and extending a foot below the narrow.

2. Cross wide end over narrow and turn back underneath.

3. Bring up and turn down through loop.

4. Pass wide end around front from left to right.

5. Then up through loop, and down through knot in front.

6. Tighten carefully and draw up to collar.

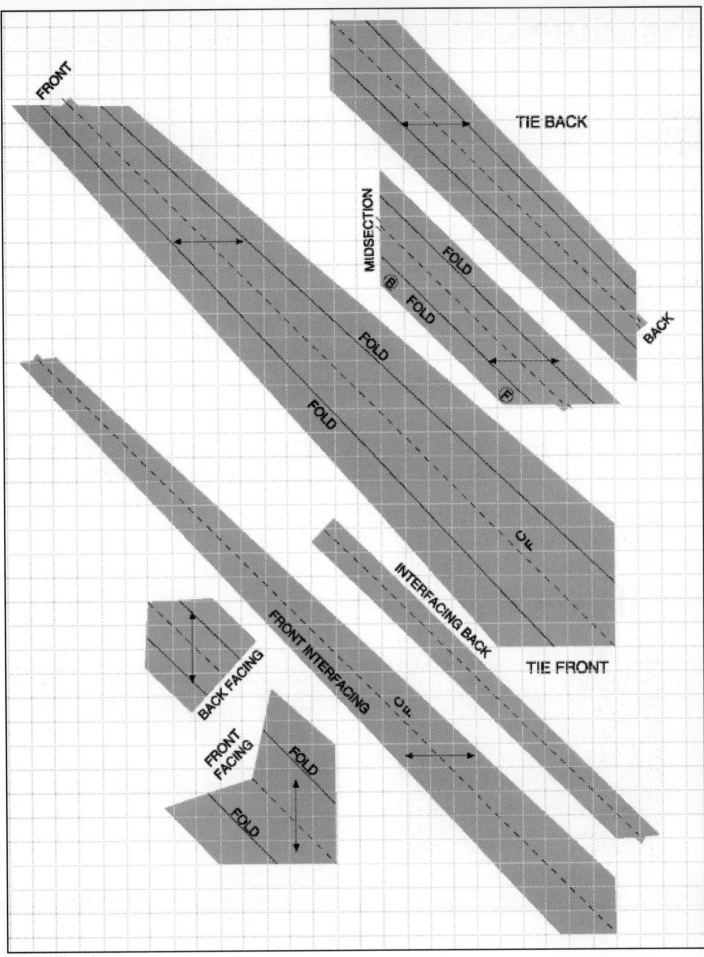

FRONT

TIE BACK

MIDSECTION

FOLD

FOLD

FOLD

FOLD

BACK

FOLD

INTERFACING BACK

OL

TIE FRONT

FRONT INTERFACING

OL

BACK FACING

FRONT FACING

FOLD

FOLD

Pattern is 25% actual size.

Standing Collar

Standing collars have no fold-over and range from about one inch wide to as much as four inches in some of the more outrageous styles. The size was determined by the width and style of the necktie or cravat, and the widest styles would be more likely seen on a young dandy than in normal fashion. Standing collars usually buttoned on to the neckband of the wearer's shirt.

Fabric Suggestions

- Medium weight woven fabrics

Materials

- ½ yard fabric
- ⅛ yard interfacing
- Collar studs

Pattern Pieces

- Collar (cut 2 fabric, 1 interfacing)

Construction

- Following the instructions on page 3, enlarge pattern piece and cut.
- Apply interfacing to the wrong side of face fabric.
- With right sides together, stitch around the entire collar leaving a 3-inch space at the center of the neck edge through which to turn the collar. Clip curves and corners, turn and press well. Slipstitch the opening closed.
- Make buttonholes where indicated.
- Attach to collarless shirt with collar studs.

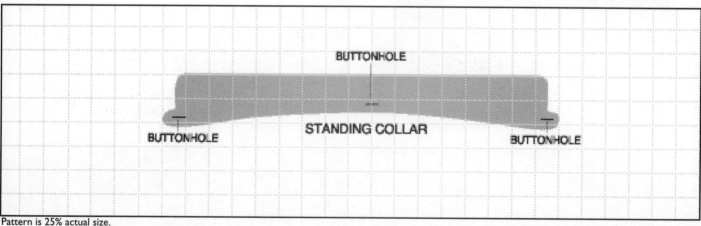

Pattern is 25% actual size.

Formal or Winged Collar

A part of men's formalwear, this standing collar is worn with corners folded down. Before the 1920s the wing collar was not just for formal wear, but was often worn for business as well. After the 1920s the winged collar was no longer a separate garment, but attached to the tuxedo shirt.

Fabric Suggestions

- Medium weight woven fabrics and cotton piques

Materials

- ½ yard fabric
- ⅛ yard interfacing
- Collar studs

Pattern Pieces

- Collar (cut 2 fabric, 1 interfacing)

Construction

- Following the instructions on page 3, enlarge pattern piece and cut.
- Apply interfacing to wrong side of fabric.
- With right sides together, stitch around the entire collar leaving a 3-inch space at the center of the neck edge through which to turn the collar. Clip curves and corners, turn and press well. Slipstitch the opening closed.
- Stitch along fold lines as indicated. Press wings down.
- Make buttonholes where indicated.
- Attach to collarless shirt with collar studs.

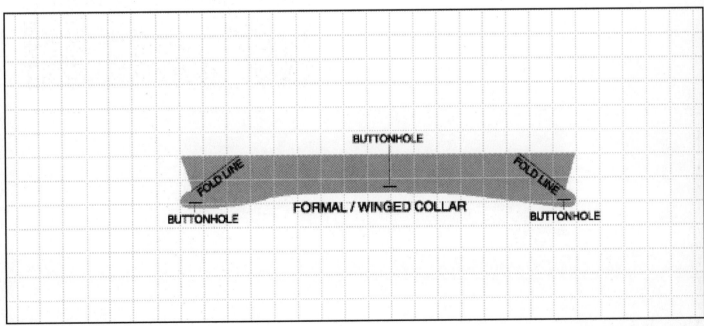

Pattern is 25% actual size.

Rounded or Hoover Collar_____

A separate article attached to the shirt at the center back and center front, these collars were originally of linen stiffened with starch and later made of paper. Very popular in the 1890s they completely fell out of fashion during the 1930s.

Fabric Suggestions

• Medium weight woven fabric, cottons, or cotton-poly blends

Materials

• ⅓ yard fabric
• ¼ yard interfacing, preferably woven, fusible or not
• Collar studs

Pattern Pieces

• Collar (cut 2 fabric, 1 interfacing)

Construction

• Following the instructions on page 3, enlarge pattern piece and cut.
• Apply interfacing to the wrong side of the face fabric.
• With right sides together, stitch around the entire collar leaving a 3-inch space through which to turn. Clip curves and corners, turn and press well. Slipstitch the opening closed.
• Topstitch around the collar.
• Stitch along fold line as indicated.
• Make buttonholes where indicated.
• Attach to collarless shirt with collar studs.

Note: If doing a limited run, you could make these collars out of white poster board and reinforce the button holes with white tape.

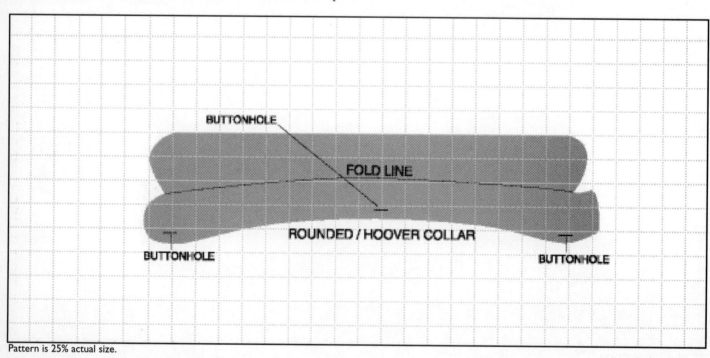

Pattern is 25% actual size.

Gladstone Collar

$\Large{T}$his collar has points flaring out at the side front and is worn with a silk cravat. Named for William Ewart Gladstone, Prime Minister of England in the late 19th century, it is a useful collar for many of the plays based on the works of Charles Dickens. In an exaggerated scale, this is the collar worn by the Mad Hatter in the Tenniel illustrations for *Alice in Wonderland.*

Fabric Suggestions

• Medium weight woven cotton, or cotton-poly blends, or linen

Materials

• ⅓ yard fabric
• ¼ yard stiff, woven, iron-on interfacings

Pattern Pieces

• Collar (cut 2 fabric, 1 interfacing)

Construction

• Following the instructions on page 3, enlarge pattern piece and cut.
• Apply interfacing to the wrong side of the face fabric.
• With right sides together, stitch around the entire collar leaving a 3-inch space through which to turn. Clip curves and corners, turn and press well. Slipstitch the opening closed.
• Topstitch around the collar.
• If using collar pins, work buttonholes where indicated. You could also use snaps or Velcro to attach the collar to a shirt.

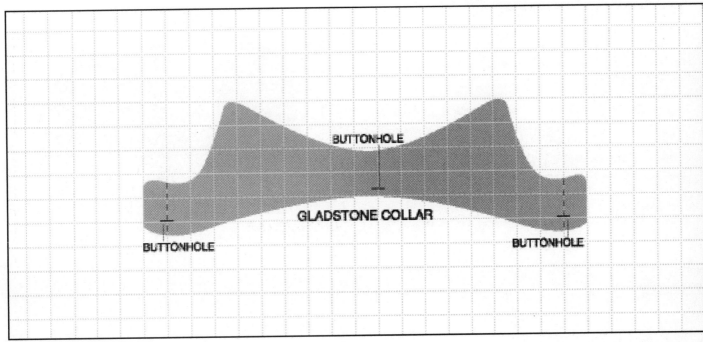

Pattern is 25% actual size.

Van Dyck or Falling Band Collar____

A collar so named because it is frequently shown in the portraits of the Flemish artist Anthony Van Dyck. It is a large collar, originally made of linen and lace, and is appropriate for many productions such as *Cyrano de Bergerac*, *Elizabeth the Queen*, or many of Shakespeare's plays. We offer two styles, one with and one without pleats. If you have an edging or trim that does not curve easily, or if you are using a directional fabric, choose the pleated version.

Fabric Suggestions

- Light to medium weight woven linen, cotton, or cotton blends

Materials

- ½ yard fabric
- ½ yard woven interfacing (if desired)
- 1⅛ yard lace for edging, preferably a Venice or some other shaped, dimensional lace
- 1 yard 2" bias strip or 1" double fold bias tape

Pattern Pieces

- Collar (cut 1 fabric, 1 lining)

Construction

- Following the instructions on page 3, enlarge pattern pieces and cut.
- For the pleated version, lightly mark darts on the wrong side of the collar. Stitch pleats into the collar piece as indicated. Press pleats toward center back of collar.
- Stitch pleats into lining piece as indicated. Press pleats toward the center front of lining.
- With right sides together, stitch around sides and bottom edge of collar and lining, leaving the neck edge open. Clip corners and curves, turn right sides out and press. Baste the neck edge closed, matching seam allowances and center back marks.
- Apply any desired lace edgings around the bottom curve and up the front edges.
- Cut a 2-inch wide piece of bias to the length of the collar neck edge (including trims) plus seam allowances. Pin bias along curved neck edge of collar, extending past trims at center fronts. Stitch ½ inch in. Fold back the seam allowances at each end of the bias strip. Press.
- Fold bias strip over raw edges of collar, folding raw edge of bias as well—this way the raw edges of the collar and the bias are all encased. Hand sew the bias in place on the back side. Add snaps to attach the collar to the garment, or baste onto the garment.

Note: For unpleated version, simply disregard instructions pertaining to pleats.

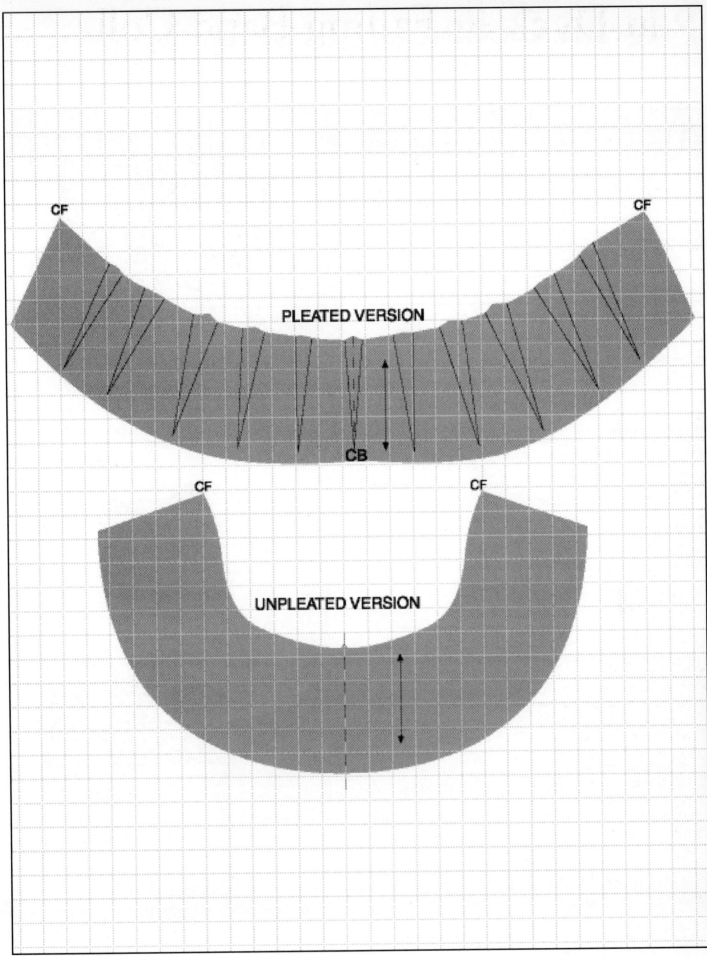

PLEATED VERSION

CF

CF

CB

UNPLEATED VERSION

CF

CF

Pattern is 25% actual size.

Pilgrim Collar

This is the collar worn by the English Colonists who settled in Plymouth in 1620. The Quakers, Puritans, and Round Heads also wore this shape collar. It should be remembered that the Puritans dressed in the fashion silhouette of their time, albeit in a more austere, simplified version. This collar is appropriate for your Thanksgiving pageant or theatrical production of *The Crucible*.

Fabric Suggestions

• Linen, cotton

Materials

• ½ yard fabric
• ½ yard interfacing

Pattern Pieces

• Collar front (cut 4 fabric, 2 interfacing)
• Collar back (cut 2 fabric, 1 interfacing)

Construction

• Following the instructions on page 3, enlarge pattern pieces and cut.
• Attach interfacing to the wrong side of two front pieces and 1 back piece. These will become the outside of the collar.
• With right sides together, stitch shoulder seams of the interfaced pieces. Repeat with the non-interfaced fronts and back. (This will become the lining of the collar.)
• With right sides together, sew the lining to the collar leaving a 3-inch space through which to turn the collar. Clip corners and curves, turn right side out and press. Slipstitch the opening closed.
• Add ties or hook and eye center front.

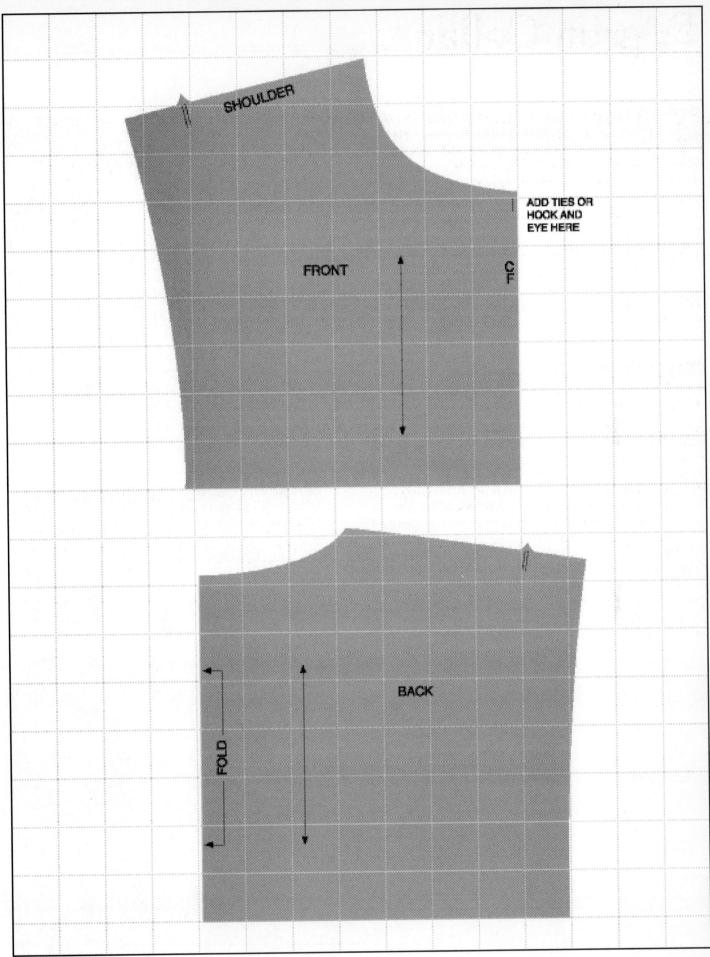

SHOULDER

FRONT

ADD TIES OR
HOOK AND
EYE HERE

C
F

BACK

FOLD

Pattern is 50% actual size.

Egyptian Collar

This Egyptian collar pattern is a costume conceit, meant to look like the heavy collars made of cylindrical beads worn by Egyptian rulers and depicted in tomb paintings and sculptures of gods and goddesses. It would be used in productions such as *Aida*, *Caesar and Cleopatra*, or *Antony and Cleopatra*.

Fabric Suggestions

- Lames, brocades, leather, pleather

Materials

- ½ yard face fabric
- ½ yard sturdy fabric for interfacing
- ½ yard lining
- Velcro

Pattern Pieces

- Collar (cut 1 fabric, 1 lining, and 1 interfacing)

Construction

- Following the instructions on page 3, enlarge pattern piece and cut.
- Flat line collar piece to interfacing
- Decorate collar as desired.
- With right sides together, pin collar to lining. Stitch around the neck edge, outside edge, and one of the center back edges. Leave one center back edge open to allow for turning. Clip curves and corners, turn right sides out and press.
- Fold seam allowances of the open edge into the collar and stitch closed.
- Sew on Velcro as indicated.
- Finish trimming as desired.

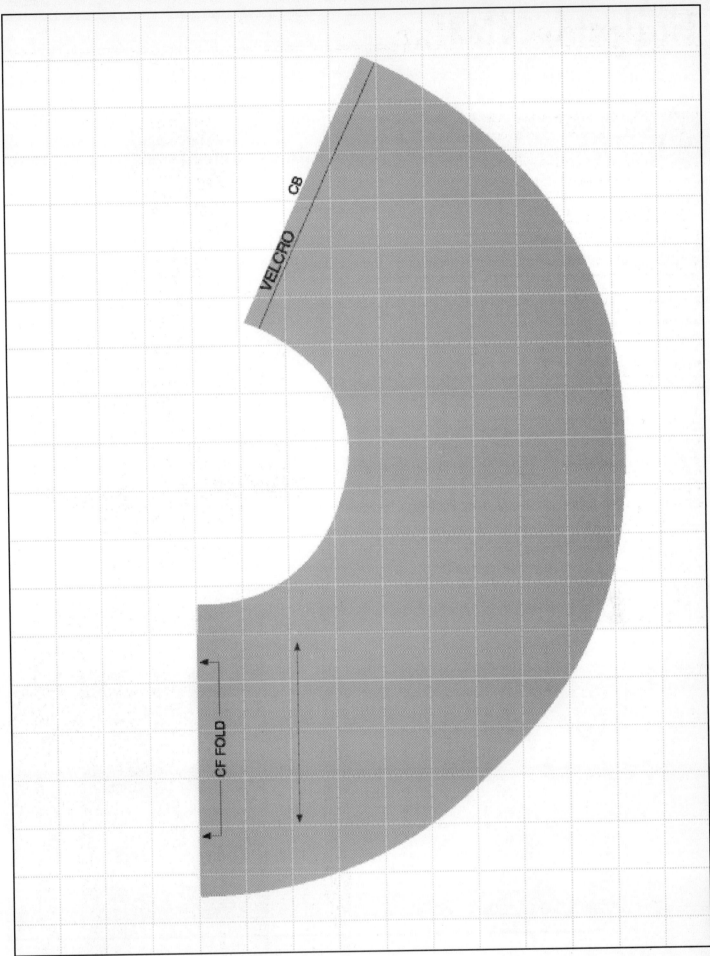

Pattern is 50% actual size.

Sailor Collar

A collar of two thicknesses of fabric with a square back and tapering to a "V" in front, the shape and the name of this collar are based on the style found on the middy sailor shirt of the United States Navy. These collars are often trimmed with braid and worn with a scarf tied underneath. The scarf is sometimes cut in one with the collar as in this pattern. These collars were very popular in the later Victorian era on women's outing costumes and on children's clothes.

Fabric Suggestions

- Medium weight woven fabrics such as cotton and cotton/polyester blends

Materials

- 1 yard fabric
- 1 yard interfacing
- Trim if desired

Pattern Pieces

- Collar (cut 2 fabric, 1 interfacing)

Construction

- Following the instructions on page 3, enlarge pattern piece and cut.
- Attach interfacing to wrong side of fabric.
- With right sides together, sew around the collar leaving a 3-inch space at the center back of the neck edge to turn. Clip the corners and curves, turn right side out and press. Slipstitch the opening closed.
- Topstitch if desired.
- Trim if desired.

Costume sketch by Arnold S. Levine for Minnie Fay in *Hello Dolly*.

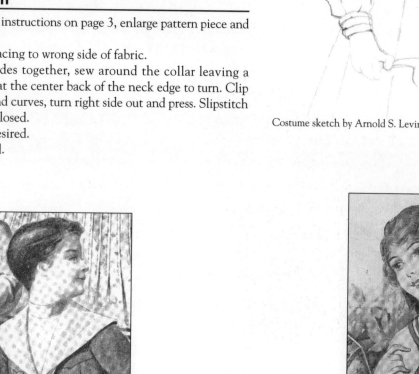

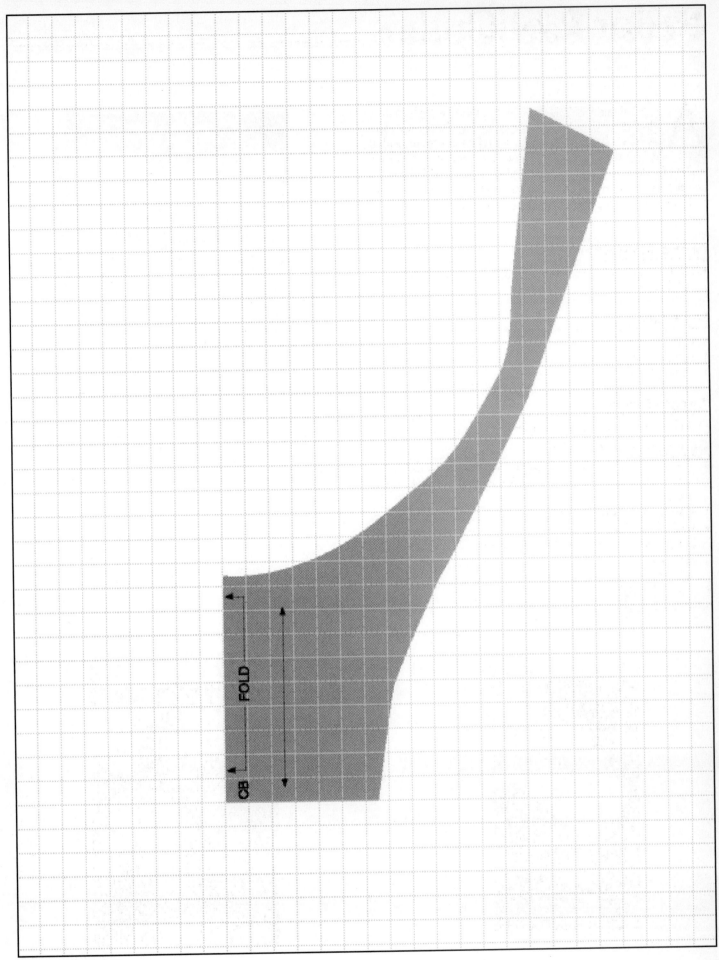

Pattern is 25% actual size.

Peter Pan Collar

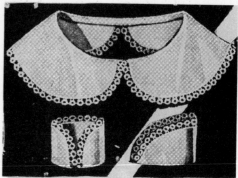

A collar named for the character of Peter Pan in a play of that name by James Barrie, it is turned down and has rounded ends. This collar was quite popular on little boys clothing in the 19th century, and on ladies' clothing in the 20th century. A larger scale version of this collar is often used on artists' smocks. The collar could also be basted to the neckline of sweater or dress with round neck.

Fabric Suggestions

• Light weight woven fabrics

Materials

• ½ yard fabric
• ½ yard interfacing (preferably woven)
• 2 inches of ¼" ribbon
• 1 shank button, ½"

Pattern Pieces

• Collar (cut 2 fabric, 1 interfacing)

Construction

• Following the instructions on page 2 enlarge pattern piece and cut.
• Attach interfacing to wrong side of face fabric.
• To make loop, fold ribbon in half bringing the 2 ends together to form a loop. Sew this to the right side of the collar as indicated.
• With right sides together, sew around the collar leaving a 3-inch space at the center back of the neck edge to turn. Clip corners and curves, turn and press. Slipstitch the opening closed.
• Topstitch if desired.
• Sew button on left side of the collar as indicated.

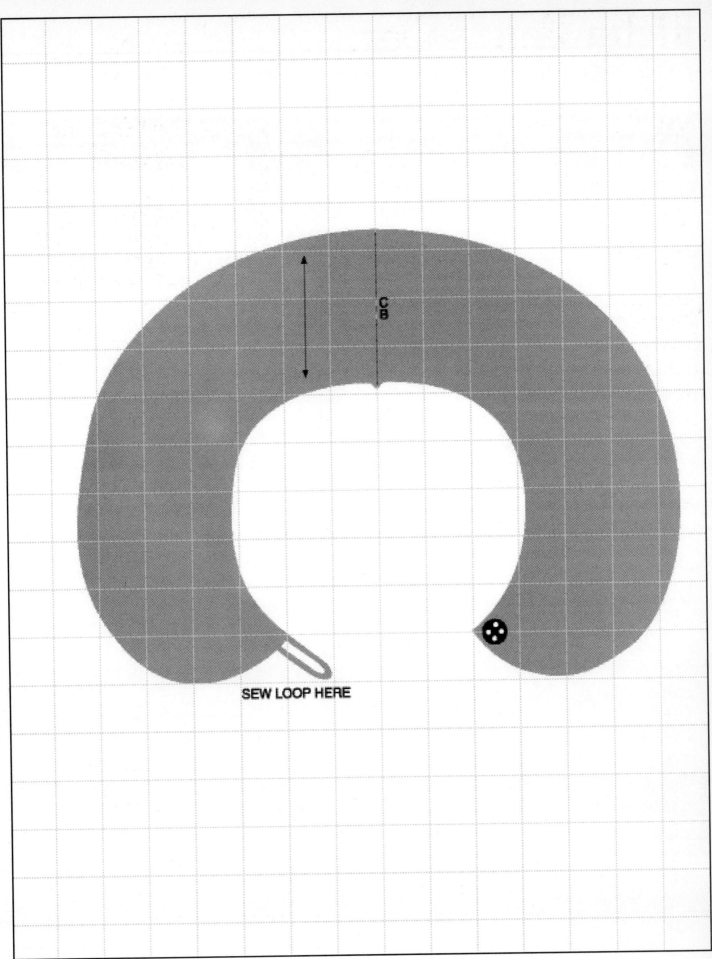

C
B

SEW LOOP HERE

Pattern is 50% actual size.

Fichu

A fichu is a scarf or shawl draped over the shoulders and tied or tucked in front. Seen as early as the 1700s it was used through the years to cover the décolletage. It is usually made of a sheer fabric.

Fabric Suggestions

- Voile, organza, organdy, lace

Materials

- ⅔ yard fabric
- Ruffle or lace trim as desired

Pattern Pieces

- Fischu (cut 1)

Construction

- Following the instructions on page 3, enlarge pattern pieces and cut.
- Finish edges with rolled hem.
- Attach trim to the outer edge as desired.

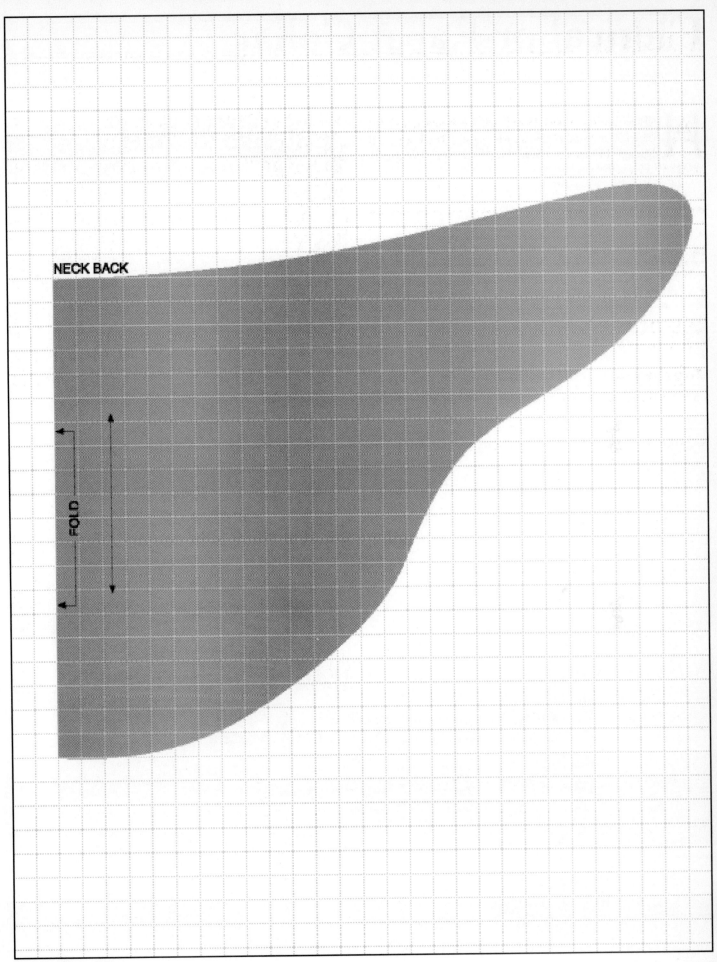

NECK BACK

FOLD

Pattern is 25% actual size.

Clerical or Rabat Collar

Historically, this style of turned down collar falling over the chest was worn by gentlemen in the 15th and 16th centuries. It was later adapted into this clerical collar with two short chest lappets. It is worn by Anglican clergy in Britain and Episcopal priests in America.

Fabric Suggestions

- Medium weight wovens, usually white or natural

Materials

- ¾ yard fabric
- ½ yard interfacing

Pattern Pieces

- Lappets (cut 2 fabric, 2 lining) **Note:** Cut one left and one right lappet by flipping pattern over.
- Band (cut 1 fabric, 1 lining)

Construction

- Following the instructions on page 3, enlarge pattern pieces and cut.
- With right sides together, stitch around one lappet and its lining, leaving the top edge open. Repeat with second lappet. Clip corners, turn right sides out and press.
- With right sides together, pin lappets to each side of collar centerline as indicated on pattern. Stitch lappets to collar band.
- With right sides together, place collar band lining over the collar band. Stitch top and sides of the band. Clip the corners and turn right side out.
- Fold the seam allowances at the bottom of the collar band and the lining into the band. Hand sew the opening closed.
- Add ties, Velcro or buttons and buttonholes to center back as desired.

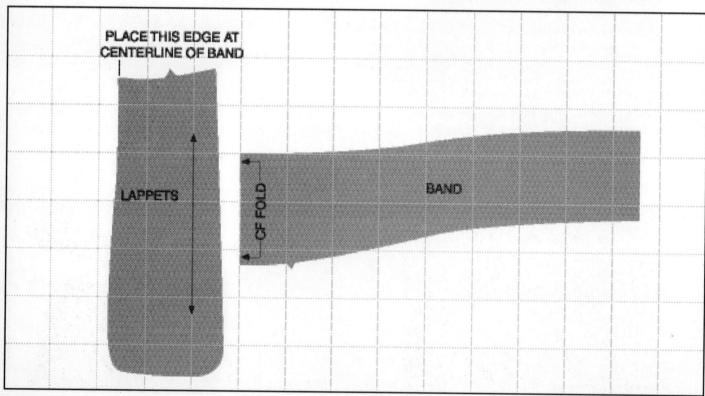

PLACE THIS EDGE AT CENTERLINE OF BAND

LAPPETS

CF FOLD

BAND

Pattern is 50% actual size.

Falling Ruff

This soft pleated ruff falls from the neck onto the shoulders and is appropriate for clowns, Pierrot and Pierette, as well as Elizabethan and Cavalier gentlemen.

Fabric Suggestions

- Lawn, organdy, cotton, broadcloth, handkerchief linen, usually white or off-white. Avoid fabric with an obvious right and wrong side.

Materials

- Fabric—yardage varies according to depth of ruffle and size of neck
- 1½ yard ¼" ribbon or long shoelaces for ties
- snaps
- Lace edging (optional)
- Grosgrain ribbon #5 or ⅞" petersham the desired length of the ruff

Pattern Pieces

- Neck band as described below (cut 1)
- Ruff body as described below (cut 1)

Note: Measurements for rectangular pattern pieces are described below. No scaled pattern pieces are provided.

Construction

- Neckband: Determine if the ruff is to be worn directly on the neck of the actor or is to be worn on a doublet or other piece of clothing. Measure desired length of neckband and cut the petersham to that length plus one inch. Turn over ½ inch on each end and press.
- Ruff body: Cut a piece of fabric twice the desired depth of the ruff plus 1-inch seam allowance. (Depth is the distance from the neck out). This piece of fabric should be three times the length of the petersham previously cut, or two times the length for heavier fabrics.
- Find the center of the fabric strip and press lengthwise. Put in gathering stitches ⅜ inch out from either side of this centerline.

- Hem the long sides of this fabric strip—hem one edge going toward one side of the fabric and the other edge to the other side of the fabric.
- If you wish to add a lace edging or trims to the ruff, do it now. Again, like the hem, one to one side and one to the other.
- Pull the gathering stitches to fit the fabric onto the ribbon. Spread the gathers out evenly. Place the fabric onto the neckband with the folded back seam allowances next to the fabric. Pin fabric to neckband.
- Stitch gathered fabric to the top and bottom edges of the neckband to form a casing.
- Run a tie through the casing you have just made, leaving equal lengths on each side. These will be used to tie the ruff around the neck.
- Stitch a snap at the outside edges of the ruff to keep it closed.

Circular Ruff

Wheel-shaped pleated collars were worn in 16th and 17th centuries. Made of stiff starched linen or muslin, they were frequently trimmed with lace. Historically, the ruff started as the ruffle at the top edge of a shirt or chemise neckband. By the 1550s it had become a broad gathered or pleated band, by the 1560s it moved into a formalized series of figure 8s, and by the 1590s ruffs were shoulder width and often needed to be propped up in back. Ruffs stayed in style into the 1620s.

The finished ruff has a neck measurement of 16 inches. Lengthen or shorten as necessary by cutting the petersham base the desired length plus 2 inches.

Fabric Suggestions

- Swiss mesh, nylon horsehair, heavy polyester taffeta

Materials

- ½ yard or grosgrain ribbon #5 or ⅞ inch petersham
- 1½ yard fabric
- 9 yards lace edging
- hooks and bars for closures
- 4 yards ½" single fold bias tape
- snaps

Pattern Pieces

- Circular ruff (cut 6). If your neck is larger than 16", you may need to cut an additional circle.

Construction

- Following the instructions on page 3, enlarge pattern piece and cut.
- Neckband: Cut a piece of ribbon or petersham 18 inches long. Hem the two raw edges with a small double-fold hem. The ribbon should now measure 17 inches.
- Ruffle: With right sides together, stitch two of the circular ruffle pieces together along the slit edges, sewing the A side of one circle to the B side of another. (As you sew the circles together, make sure that all of the smaller [neck] edges are on the same side.) Repeat with all pieces until you have one very long ruffle.
- Roll hem, bind the outer edge, or apply lace edging or other trim to the outer edge at this time.
- Hem the two extreme ends of the ruffle.

Traditional Method (cartridge pleats)

- Sew hooks and bars to the ribbon with a 1-inch overlap.
- Bind the neck edge of the ruffle with bias tape.
- Mark the neck edge with marks 1½ inches apart. With a heavy weight thread, sew a long running stitch, coming in and out at the marked intervals. Pull up on this thread, making accordion pleats, until ruffle measures 16 inches. Make sure the pleats are even and stitch to the top and the bottom of the ribbon.

- Decoratively arrange figure 8s at the outside edge of the ruff and tack each eight to its neighbor.
- Stitch a small snap to the outer edges of the ruff to join it together.

Simplified Method (flat pleats)

- Make one-inch (or desired size) box pleats the neck edge of the ruffle.
- Stitch pleats in place.
- Fold neckband in half lengthwise. Encase raw edge of pleats in the ribbon and stitch through.
- Add hooks and eyes to the ribbon.
- Arrange outer ruffle into figure 8s and tack in place.
- Stitch a small snap to the outer edges of the ruff to join it together.

These illustrations are variations on the circular ruff. The pattern will make a ruff that looks most like the one shown above.

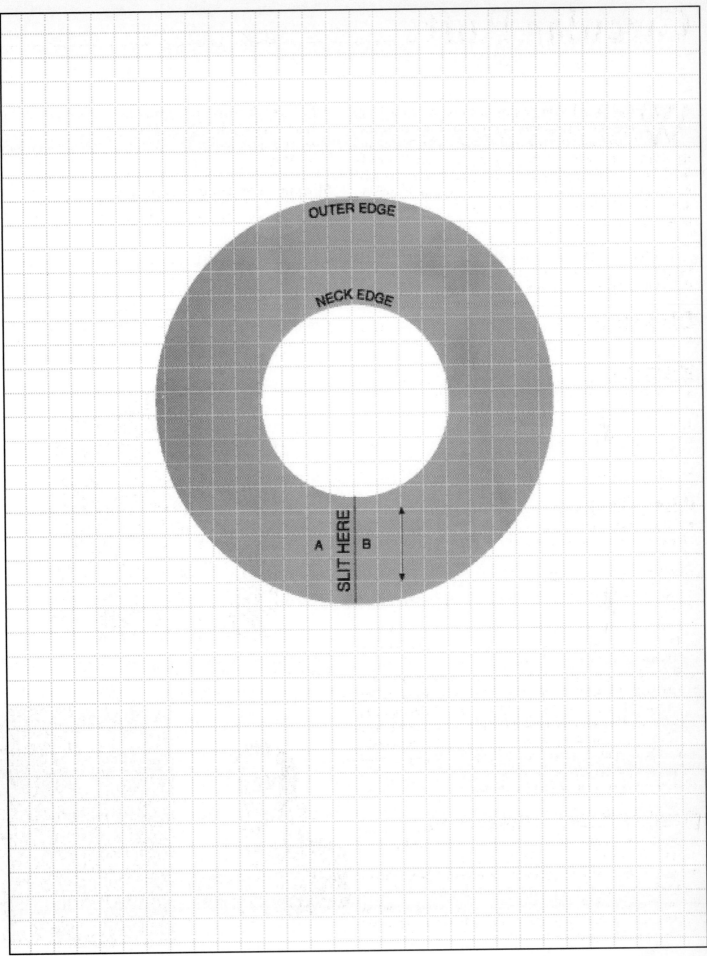

Pattern is 25% actual size.

Chapter 3

BELTS & APRONS

Victorian Belt

Victorian women wore a form-fitting shaped belt, stiffened to hold its shape, often with a front point extending down from the natural waist. This variation opens in the center back, but they also opened on the side. These belts were in style when the waist of fashion was at the natural waist of the wearer. Use these belts for the women's costumes in *The Music Man*, *Hello Dolly*, or any play set around the turn of the 20th century.

Fabric Suggestions

- Any decorative fabric to go with the costume

Materials

- ½ yard fabric
- ½ yard canvas or drill (for inner layer)
- ½ yard lining fabric
- Feather boning or steel boning and casings

Pattern Pieces

- Front (cut 1 fabric, 1 lining with seam allowances, and 1 inner-layer without seam allowances on the top and bottom)
- Back (cut 2 fabric, 2 lining with seam allowances, and 2 inner-layer with out seam allowances on the top and bottom)

Construction

- Following the instructions on page 3, enlarge pattern pieces and cut.
- With right sides together, stitch side seams in fabric, in inner layer, and in lining. Press seams open.
- Stitch boning or boning casing over the side seams of the inner layer. Stitch boning or boning casing on the inner layer at the center front and side front as indicated.
- Insert bones into casings.
- With the boning side up, place the inner layer on the wrong side of the face fabric, matching side seams. Baste in place. Clip curves and press seam allowance up over the inner layer.
- Stitch along stitch line of lining piece. Clip curves and press seam allowance back.
- Pin lining to backside of belt, curving belt away from table surface while pinning—this will make the lining slightly smaller than the outside of the belt and will keep it from bunching when wrapped around the waist. Slip stitch lining to belt.
- Add closures to the back as desired.
- Remove basting threads.

Costume design by Arnold S. Levine for Varya in *The Cherry Orchard*.

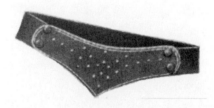

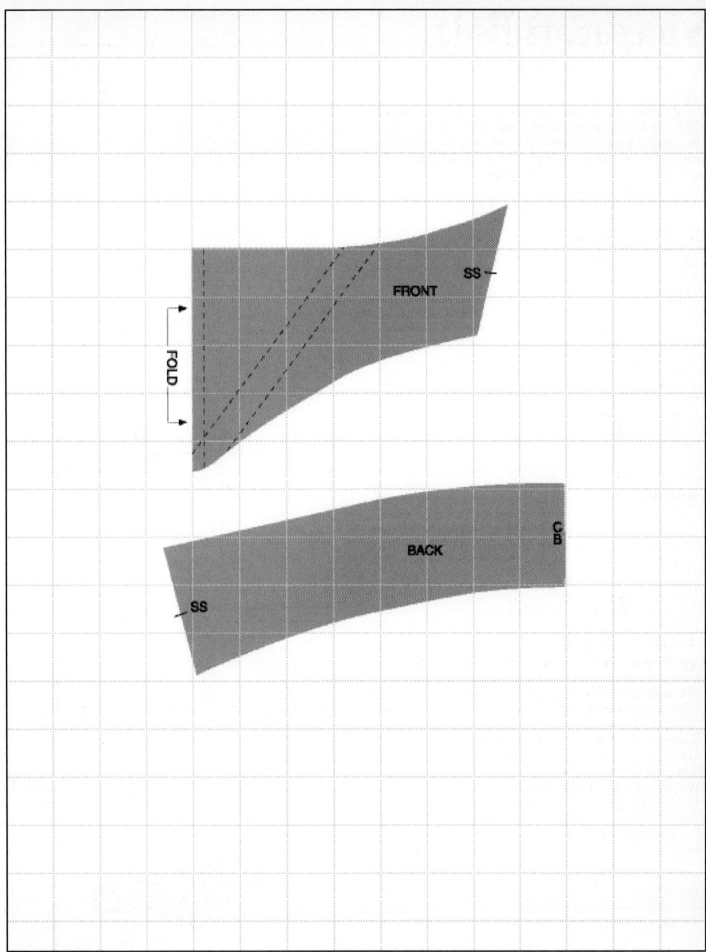

FOLD

FRONT

SS

BACK

C
B

SS

Pattern is 50% actual size.

Shaped Belt

This curved belt sits with the top edge at the natural waistline and extends down. This was a very popular style in the 1950s and would make a great accessory for *Grease*, *The Pajama Game*, *Damn Yankees*, or plays such as *Picnic* or *A Hatful Of Rain*. This pattern also works well with low-riding, hip hugger pants or skirts. This belt fits a woman with a 30-inch high hip measurement.

Fabric Suggestions

- Leather, heavy vinyl, any fabric bonded to a sturdy base

Materials

- ⅓ yard fabric
- ⅓ yard buckram or heavy nonwoven interfacing
- ⅓ yard lining
- 1 large snap

Pattern Pieces

- Belt (cut 1 of heavy weight non-fraying material; or cut 1 fabric with seam allowance, 1 stiffening piece with no seam allowance, 1 Stitch Witchery with seam allowances, 1 lining with seam allowance

Construction

- Following the instructions on page 3, enlarge pattern piece and cut.
- If using a thin fabric, lay fabric piece face down on ironing surface. Lay Stitch Witchery on top, then the stiffening piece.
- Using the tip of a hot iron, heat set the stiffening piece to the fabric in a number of places to keep it from shifting, being careful not to get any Stitch Witchery on the iron.
- Clip corners and curves just to the edge of the stiffening piece. Starting on one of the long sides of the belt, press seam allowance of the fabric and Stitch Witchery to the back of the stiffening piece. This is best done using the side of the iron. Continue around the entire shape until the belt and backing is bonded together. Flip to right side of belt and press to make sure there are no air pockets.
- If your lining is of a non-raveling fabric, cut to shape and bond to wrong side of belt.

Note: While the belt is warm from bonding, if you roll it as you would around the body, the bonding will help to hold the shape.

- If your lining fabric is a thin woven fabric, fold back your seam allowances and press in place. Lay lining on back of belt and sew together.

- If using leather or a sturdy non-raveling material, cut to shape with no seam allowances.
- Add snaps, grippers, or hooks and eyes for closures. The belt could also be cut smaller than the actor's waist and grommets or eyelets added to tie together.

Costume sketch by Arnold S. Levine for *Picnic*.

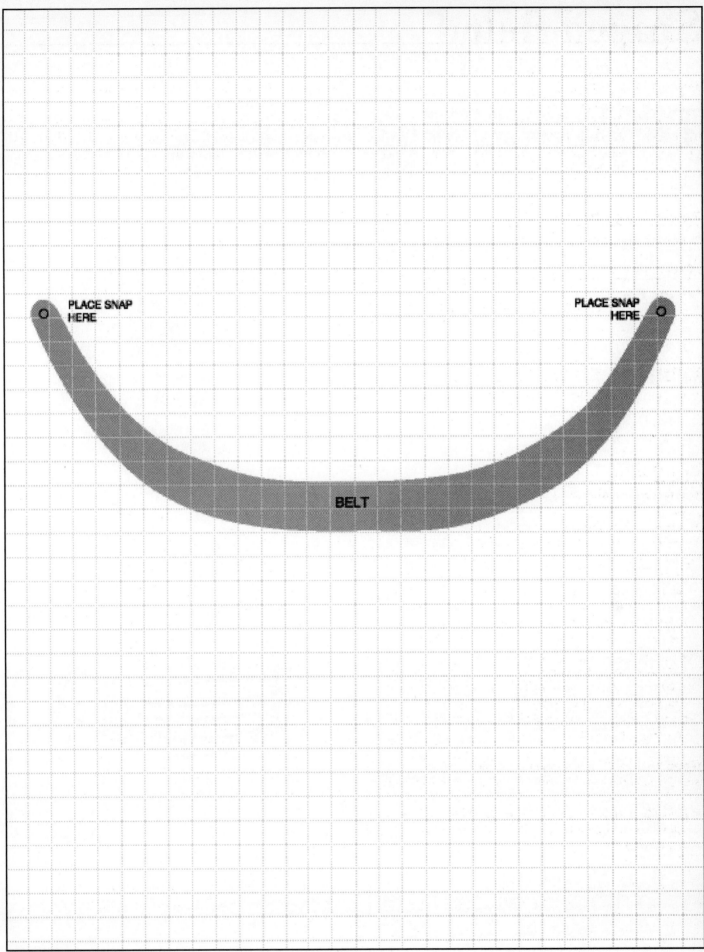

PLACE SNAP HERE

PLACE SNAP HERE

BELT

Pattern is 25% actual size.

Cummerbund

This broad waistband is usually worn in place of a vest with men's dress clothes and has been adapted for use in various styles of women's clothes. Cummerbunds are usually worn with the pleats facing up to catch crumbs of food and conceal interior pockets. The word originated in the early 17th century from the Urdu language, kamar-band, literally "loin-band, waistband."

Fabric Suggestions

- Heavyweight satin, brocade, faille, tie fabric

Pattern Pieces

- Side (cut 2 fabric)
- Front (cut 1 fabric)
- Backing (cut 1 lining)

Materials

- ½ yard fabric
- ½ yard lining
- ¼ yard interfacing
- 1 yard 1-inch elastic
- Velcro or buckles

Construction

- Following the instructions on page 3, enlarge pattern pieces and cut.
- Apply interfacing to backing piece.
- Mark fold lines on the wrong side of front piece. Press pleats as marked. Turn piece so you are looking at the backside. Stitch each pleat to itself, ¼ inch in from the folded edge—this will keep the pleats in place.
- Once all the pleats are made, pin the outside edges and stitch along seam allowance to hold in place.
- With right sides together, stitch one side piece to each side of pleated front piece. Press seam allowances toward the side pieces and topstitch in place.
- Stitch a piece of elastic to each side end, laying the elastic onto the face of the cummerbund.
- With right sides together, pin the cummerbund to the backing piece and stitch around all sides, leaving an opening on the bottom edge to turn through. Turn right sides out and gently press edges, being careful not to disturb the pleats.
- Hand stitch the opening closed.
- Add Velcro or buckles to the ends of elastic, checking for fit.

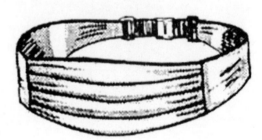

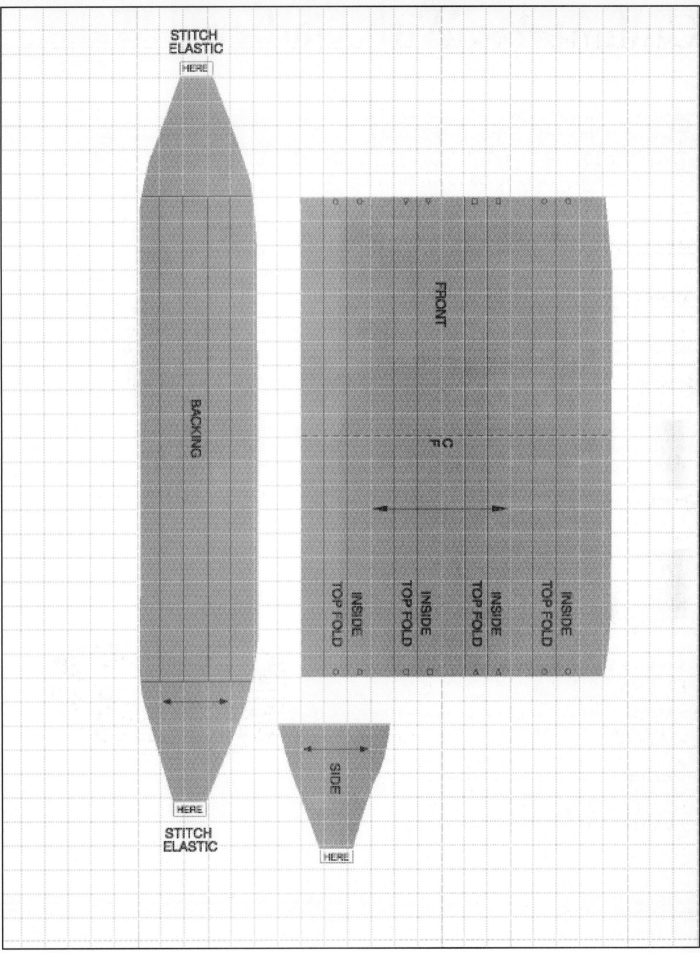

Pattern is 25% actual size.

Half Apron With Gathered Waist __

Aprons are worn over clothing to protect or adorn. Usually of cloth, plastic, or leather, aprons have been made in various shapes and sizes throughout history. From the old French word naperon, literally "small cloth," the original phrase "a naperon" was later construed as "an apron."

This apron is a simple skirt with a waist gathered onto a straight band with ties and is a basic part of ethnic folk dress and worn by working people. During the mid 1700s, these aprons might have been made of rich fabrics with lace trimming, worn by courtiers who played at being "happy peasants."

Fabric Suggestions

- Cotton, cotton blend, calico, gingham, organdy

Materials

- 1 yard fabric
- ¼ yard interfacing

Pattern Pieces

- Skirt (cut 1)
- Waistband (cut 1 face fabric, 1 interfacing)
- Pocket (cut 1 or 2 as desired)
- Ties (cut 2)

Construction

- Following the instructions on page 3, enlarge pattern pieces and cut.
- Hem sides of skirt panel. If you wish to sew on a pocket, do so now.
- Stitch two rows of machine basting at upper edge of skirt, one on the stitch line and one in the seam allowance.
- Interface the wrong side of the waistband piece.
- With right sides together, pin top edge of apron skirt to one of the long edges of the waistband, matching the center front points and side points as marked. Gather apron to fit waistband, pin, and stitch. Lightly press seam allowances toward waistband.
- Press seam allowance under on the remaining edge of waistband. Press seam allowance in at the edges. Fold waistband in half, bringing pressed edge down to the seam already stitched, encasing all raw edges. Pin.
- Fold each tie piece in half the long way (right sides together) and stitch along the side and mitered end. Clip corners, turn right sides out and press. Topstitch if desired.
- Pleat raw edge of each tie to fit ends of waistband, and stitch to side seam of the waistband.
- Stitch waistband closed along side seams and bottom along the skirt edge as previously pinned. Check length of apron. Hem as desired.

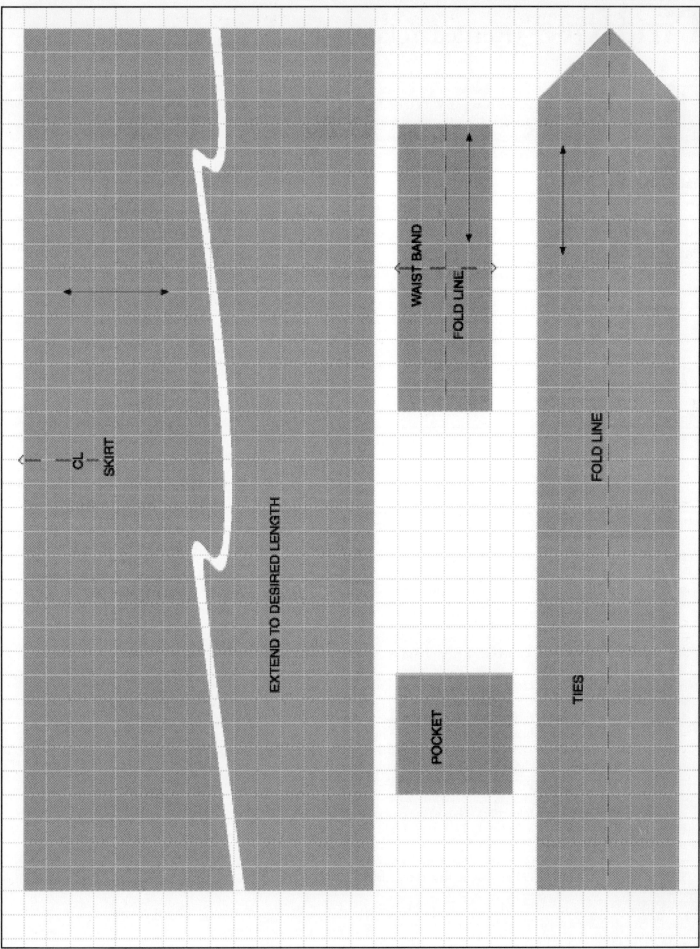

CL

SKIRT

EXTEND TO DESIRED LENGTH

WAIST BAND

FOLD LINE

POCKET

TIES

FOLD LINE

Pattern is 25% actual size.

Pinafore (Ruffled Yoke Style)

This style of apron has a bib and shoulder straps. Ruffles at the shoulders or at the hem, are optional. With the ruffle this is a wonderful Victorian maid's or little girl's apron or pinafore, perfect for *Alice in Wonderland*. A simpler version would be suitable for *Oklahoma!*, or *Fiddler on the Roof*.

Fabric Suggestions

- Cotton, cotton-polyester blends, calico, gingham, organdy, crisp sheers, eyelet.

Pattern Pieces

- Skirt front—36" × desired length (no pattern given, cut 1 on fold)
- Skirt back—18" × desired length (no pattern given, cut 2)
- Waistband (cut 1 front and 1 facing)
- Bib (cut 1)
- Shoulder straps (cut 2 fronts and 2 facings)
- Shoulder ruffle (cut 2 on fold [or cut 4])
- Ties (cut 4)
- Pockets (cut 2, optional)

Materials

- 3 yards fabric
- ¼ yard interfacing
- 2 buttons, ¾" (optional)

Construction

- Following the instructions on page 3, enlarge pattern pieces and cut.
- *Pockets (optional)*: Fold under seam allowance and 1 inch of top of pocket, press, and stitch. Starting at one end of the pocket, sew a stay-stitching line around the remaining three sides. Clip curves and press to back of pocket. Pin pockets to skirt front. Stitch close to the press line on side and bottom edges.
- *Skirt:* Sew skirt backs to skirt front at sides. Finish back edges with a small double-fold hem. Hem bottom edge of skirt or add ruffle if desired.
- *Bib:* Fold under seam allowance and 1 inch at top of bib. Press and topstitch.
- *Shoulder straps and ruffle:* With right sides together, lay shoulder straps on side seams of bib, matching top of bib with line on strap. Stitch. Turn pieces over and lay facings on top, right sides together—bib is sandwiched between straps and facings. Stitch long straight seam. Turn strap and facing right side out away from bib center. Press.

    If ruffle was not cut on fold, stitch seams where indicated. Press seam allowance open. Finish the long straight side of ruffle with a small double-fold hem. Finish the two short ends with a small double-fold hem. Gather the ruffle along the curved side by stitching two rows of machine basting, one on the stitch line and one in the seam allowance.
- With right sides together, pin ruffle to shoulder strap, being careful not to catch facing and matching the end points of the ruffle to the marks on the straps and matching the ruffle's cen-

terline to the shoulder mark on the strap. Pull up on the bobbin threads of basting stitches to gather the ruffle to fit. Adjust the fullness and stitch in place.
- Fold under seam allowance on facing and press. Pin folded edge of facing to shoulder strap, enclosing all raw edges. Slipstitch facings to shoulder straps. Topstitch if desired.
- *Waistband and Ties:* Gather upper edge of skirt by putting in two rows of machine basting, one on the stitch line and one in the seam allowance. With right sides together, pin skirt to lower edge of the waistband, stopping just before the seam allowance at each end. Match side seams and centerline of skirt to marks on waistband. Pull up on the bobbin threads of basting stitches and adjust gathers to fit. Stitch. Do not press seams open.
- Pin bib to upper edge of waistband, matching centerlines. Stitch. With bib still down over waistband and skirt, pin waistband facing over waistband. Fold back seam allowances at the ends of the waistband facing. Stitch along top edge of waistband. Press seam allowances toward skirt.
- With right sides together, stitch 2 ties around 3 sides, leaving the short straight side open. Clip corners, turn right side out and press. Repeat with other tie.
- Pleat open end of the tie to fit ends of waistband. Stitch into place. Fold the raw edges of waistband facing to wrong side. Pin to back of waistband and stitch in place, being sure to encase all raw edges of ties and skirt.
- Fit on the actor and position shoulder straps in the back, onto the waistband. Stitch as pinned or apply buttons and buttonholes.

Costume sketch by Arnold S. Levine for maids in *My Fair Lady*.

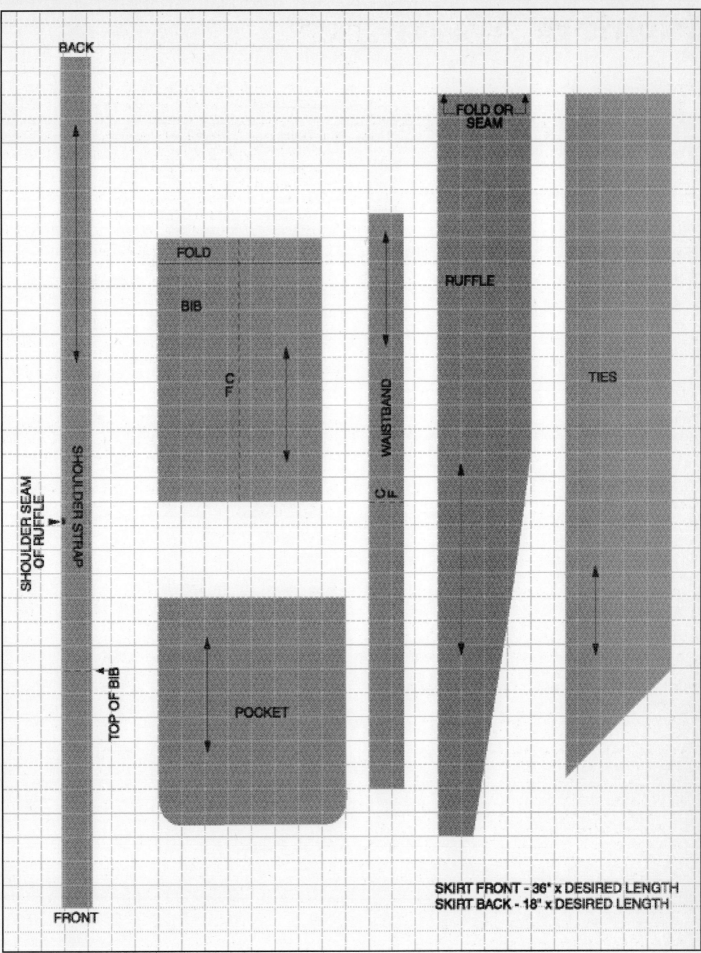

BACK

FOLD

BIB

C
F

SHOULDER SEAM
OF RUFFLE

SHOULDER STRAP

TOP OF BIB

POCKET

FRONT

WAISTBAND

C
F

FOLD OR
SEAM

RUFFLE

TIES

SKIRT FRONT - 36" x DESIRED LENGTH
SKIRT BACK - 18" x DESIRED LENGTH

Pattern is 25% actual size.

Waitress Apron

This short, small apron is the style worn by waitresses in contemporary settings. There are many shapes for this kind of apron; we have chosen a typical variation. You might use an apron of this type for productions of *Come Back to the Five and Dime, Jimmy Dean, Jimmy Dean, The Petrified Forest*, or any play with a scene in a diner or with a saucy "French Maid".

Fabric Suggestions

• Crisp cottons, cotton-polyester blends, polyester taffetas

Pattern Pieces

• Base (cut 1)
• Pocket layer (cut 1)
• Waistband (cut 1)
• Ties (cut 4)

Construction

• Following the instructions on page 3, enlarge pattern pieces and cut.
• Press in and stitch double fold hem along top, straight edges of the pocket layer.
• With right sides of pocket layer to wrong side of body, stitch together, matching scallops and points. Clip curves, turn finished sides out and press.
• Double fold the seam allowance along the sides above pocket and stitch. Continue this stitch line for topstitching around the bottom curves if desired—this makes a good sturdy finish.
• Stitch a centerline through the pocket to hold it to the apron and to create 2 pockets from the one large pocket.
• With right sides together and matching center-front marks, pin waistband to top of base and stitch. Fold in seam allowance on the other long side of the waistband. Press. Fold waistband in half lengthwise, matching seam allowance lines and press.
• Stitch one tie to each end of waistband, pleating to fit.
• From the back, fold waistband onto itself, encasing seam allowances of waistband, base and ties. Topstitch around waistband.

Costume sketch by Arnold S. Levine for Cissy in *Come Back to the Five & Dime Jimmy Dean, Jimmy Dean.*

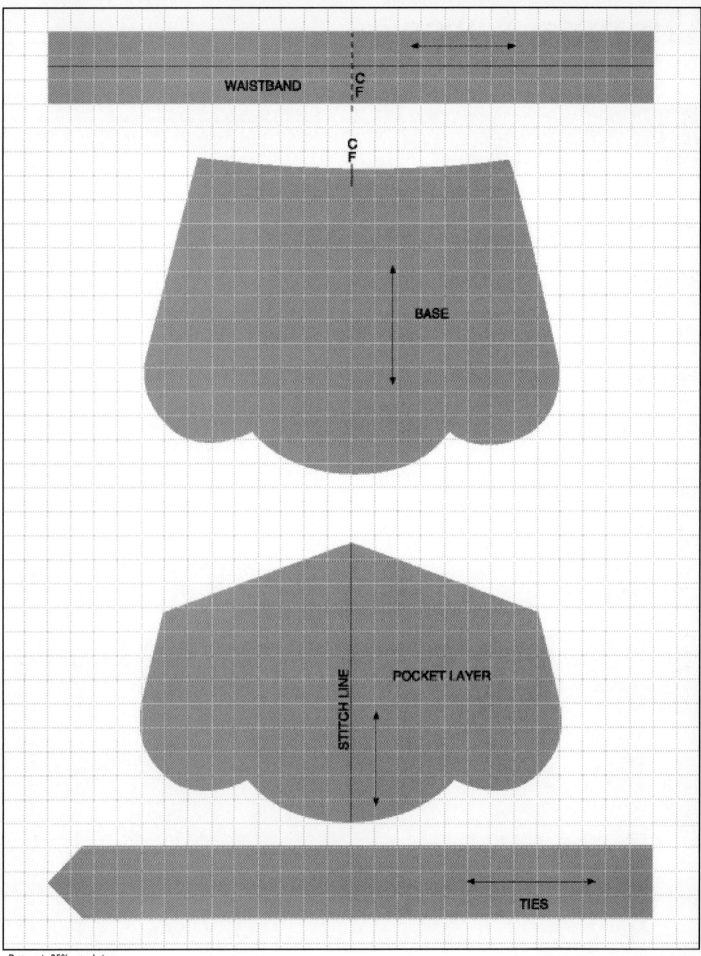

WAISTBAND

CF

CF

BASE

STITCH LINE

POCKET LAYER

TIES

Pattern is 25% actual size.

Butcher's Apron

The bib and skirt for this apron are cut in one piece. This apron in variation may be used for many types of occupations: butchers, bakers, cobblers, chefs, and waiters, among others. It is perfect for the characters of Barnaby and Cornelius in *Hello Dolly*.

Fabric Suggestions

- Heavy weight woven fabrics such as twill denim or drill

Materials

- 1½ yards fabric

Pattern Pieces

- Apron body (cut 1)
- Pocket (no pattern given, cut 1 or 2, 10½" × 8 ½")
- Neckband (no pattern given, cut 1, 3" × 27")
- Ties (no pattern given, cut 2, 3" × 45")

Construction

- Following the instructions on page 3, enlarge pattern pieces and cut.
- Fold down ½ inch at top edge of pocket and fold again. Press and stitch.
- Fold ½ inch around the other 3 sides of pocket and press. Place pocket on apron as indicated. Pin in place. Stitch around pocket ,making sure to secure the upper corners by stitching again.
- Double fold hem around the entire body of the apron.
- With right sides together stitch neck pieces together lengthwise with ½" seam allowance. Turn right side out and press. Top stitch along both long edges. Attach as indicated on pattern.
- With right sides together, stitch a tie piece lengthwise and across one short edge with ½" seam allowances. Clip corners, turn and press. Topstitch all edges of tie. Repeat with other tie. Stitch one tie at each side where indicated.

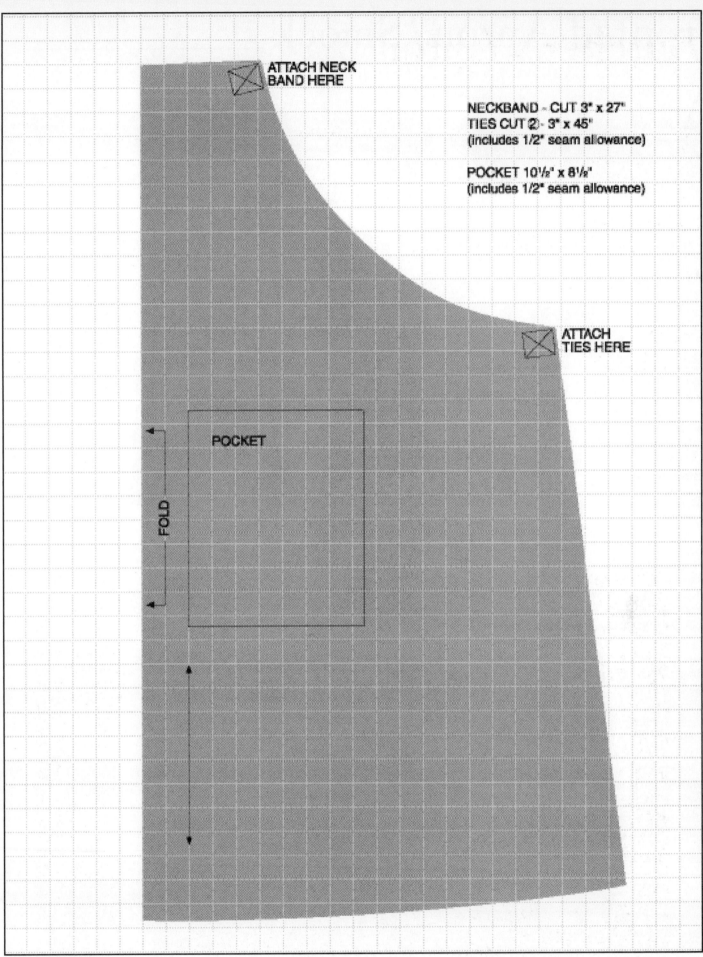

ATTACH NECK
BAND HERE

NECKBAND - CUT 3" x 27"
TIES CUT ② - 3" x 45"
(includes 1/2" seam allowance)

POCKET 10½" x 8½"
(includes 1/2" seam allowance)

ATTACH
TIES HERE

POCKET

FOLD

Pattern is 25% actual size.

Fronted Apron/Smock

A more utilitarian garment, this is an apron with a full front and sides. It slips over the head and ties in the back. A design from the early 20th century, it is still worn today. If you lengthen this apron it may be worn to depict the end of the 19th Century. This apron may be worn in any play of the 20th century that deals with working class people such as *Death of a Salesman*, *All My Sons*, or *Member of the Wedding*.

Fabric Suggestions

- Cottons, cotton blends, gingham, calico, seersucker

Materials

- 2½ yards fabric
- 9 yards ½" single fold bias binding
- 2 buttons (optional)

Pattern Pieces

- front (cut 1 on fold)
- skirt sides/back (cut 2)
- back yoke (cut 2)
- ties (cut 2)
- pocket (cut 1 or 2)

Construction

- Following the instructions on page 3, enlarge pattern pieces and cut.
- With right sides together, stitch sides to front, being sure to match bottom edges. Overlock these seams or press seam allowance toward back and topstitch.
- With right sides together, stitch back seam of back yoke. Press seam allowance to one side and topstitch.
- Sew shoulder seams, attaching apron body to back yoke Overlock these seams or press seam allowance toward back and topstitch.
- Bind neck hole with bias tape or with bias cut from fabric. Bind outer edges of apron all the way around, starting at the base of the back yoke.
- With right sides together, fold ties in half lengthwise. Stitch down the long side and across one of the short ends. Clip corners, turn ties right side out and press.
- Attach a tie to each side of the apron at the waist as indicated.
- If desired, bind outer edge of pocket(s). Pin to apron in desired position and stitch.
- Pin back yoke to skirt sides/back where indicated. Try apron on actor to assure that the position is correct. Stitch back to apron waist or attach with buttons and buttonholes.

Costume sketch by Robin L. McGee for *Pigtown* at the Irish Repertory Theatre.

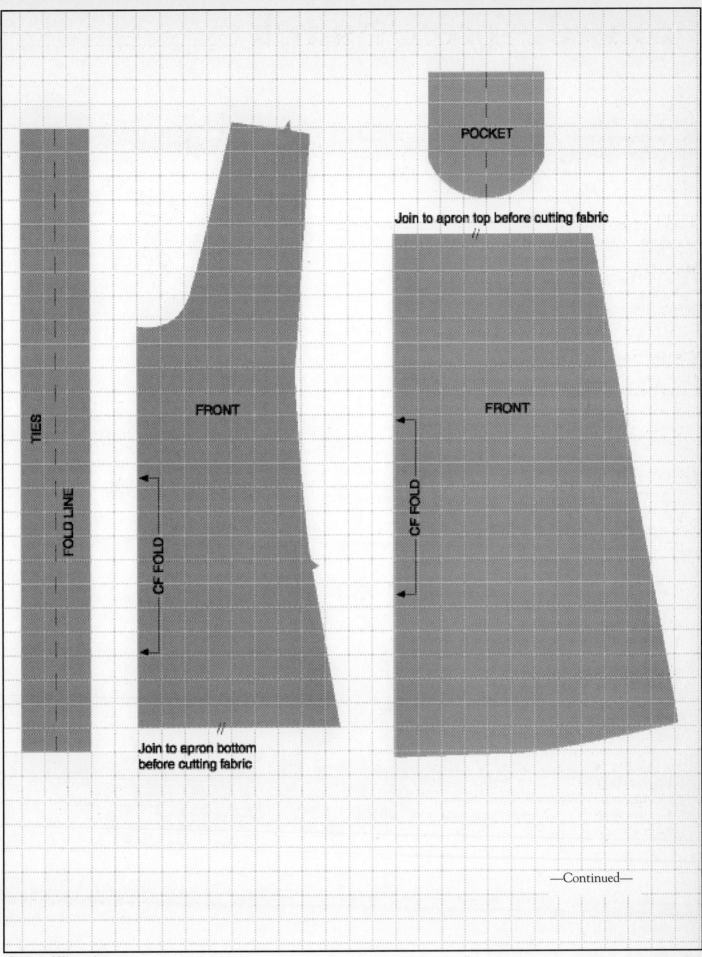

POCKET

Join to apron top before cutting fabric

FRONT

TIES

FOLD LINE

CF FOLD

FRONT

CF FOLD

Join to apron bottom
before cutting fabric

Pattern is 25% actual size.

—Continued—

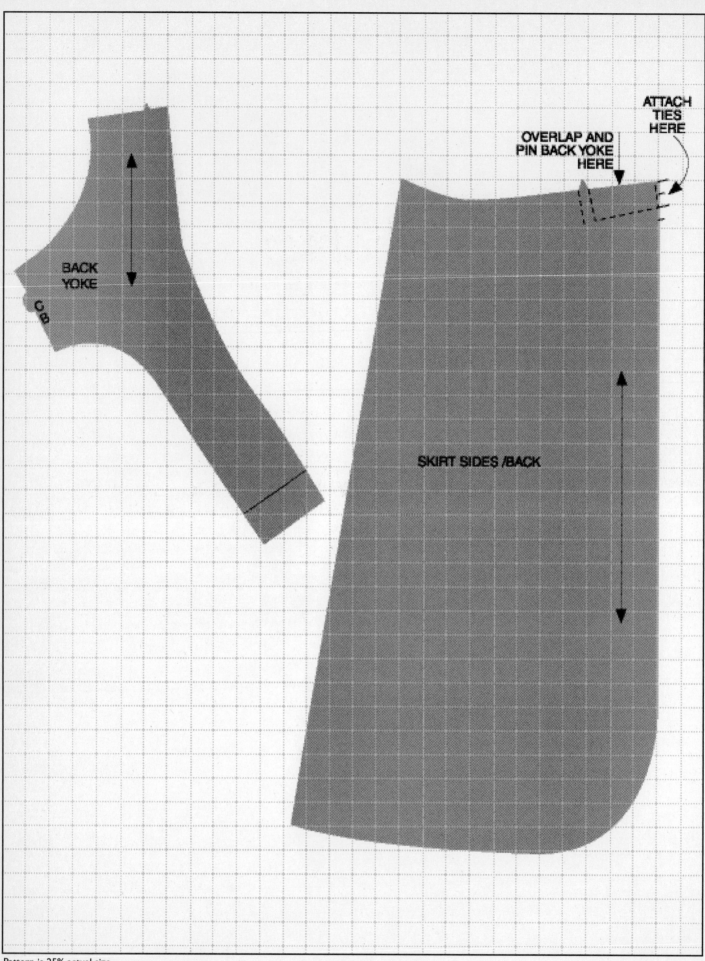

BACK
YOKE

C B

ATTACH
TIES
HERE

OVERLAP AND
PIN BACK YOKE
HERE

SKIRT SIDES /BACK

Pattern is 25% actual size.

Chapter 4

FOOTWEAR

Spats

A spat is a short cloth gaiter worn over shoes by men and women. The word "spat" is short for "spatterdash", and the garment was originally worn to protect stockings from mud splashes. These short spats were popular during the 19th and early 20th centuries and might be used in *The Boyfriend*, *Guys and Dolls*, or any of the farces by Feydeau.

Fabric Suggestions

- Wool felt, wool coating, Melton, or any fabric that will not sag and bag around the ankles

Materials

- ½ yard fabric
- ½ yard sturdy lining fabric
- 14 buttons, half inch
- ⅓ yard of 1-inch elastic

Pattern Pieces

- Inside foot (cut 2 fabric, cut 2 lining)
- Outside front (cut 2 fabric, cut 2 lining)
- Outside back (cut 2 fabric, cut 2 lining)

Construction

- Following the instructions on page 3, enlarge pattern pieces and cut.
- With right sides together, sew center front seams. Press seams open and topstitch ⅛ inch on either side of seams. Repeat with center back seams.
- Repeat this process with the lining fabric.
- With right sides together, sew lining to spat, matching seams and toe curve, and leaving straight end (where the buttons will later be placed) open. Turn right sides out and press. Turn in and stitch or bind raw edges. Topstitch around entire spat.
- Mark buttonhole placement and stitch. (You could also use Velcro for the closure. Attach the soft side of the Velcro to the overlap and the stiff side to the underlap.)
- Attach buttons. Shank buttons work best with buttonholes, flat buttons as decoration with Velcro.
- Attach 4 inches of 1-inch elastic to bottom edges as indicated. This will hold the spat to the wearer's instep.

OVERGAITERS.
FOR WOMEN.

No. 15K1211 Ladies' Fine Overgaiters, made heavy for fall and winter wear. Shoe sizes, 3 to 7. STATE SIZE. Weight, 7 ounces. No half sizes. Price, per pair....19c
No. 15K1215 Ladies' 7-button imported Kersey, the nobbiest and unexcelled overgaiter. Sizes, 3 to 7. Price, per pair..............35c

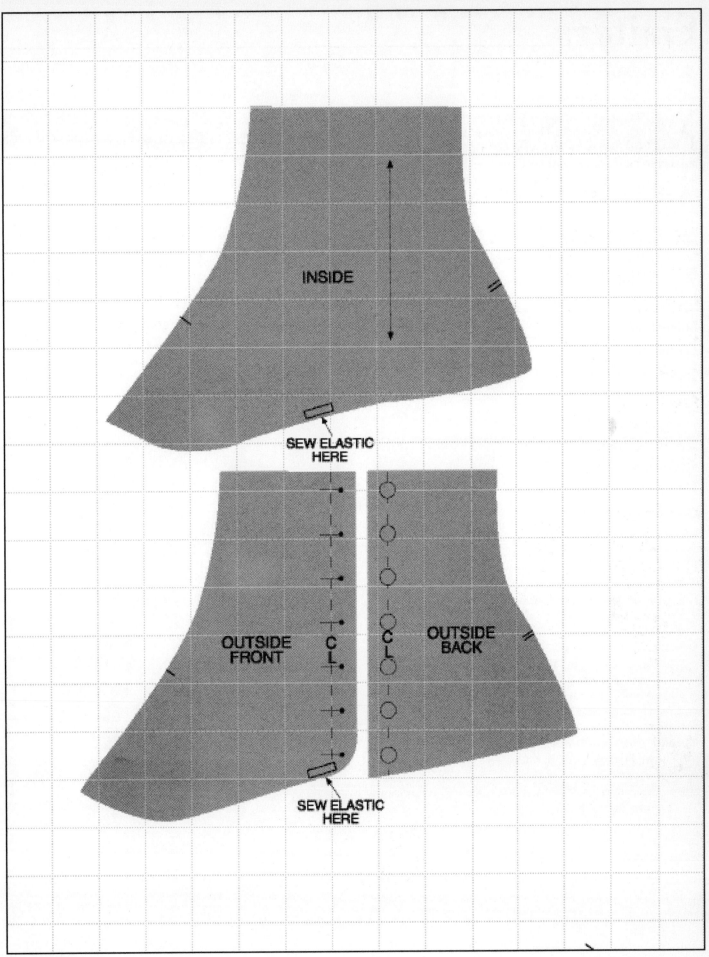

INSIDE

SEW ELASTIC
HERE

OUTSIDE
FRONT

C
L

C
L

OUTSIDE
BACK

SEW ELASTIC
HERE

Pattern is 50% actual size.

Gaiters

Made of cloth or leather, gaiters cover the leg from the instep to the knee. They are closed up the side and are often secured with a strap under the ankle. Worn with military uniforms or for hunting, these would be good accessories for any play set during the American Revolution or the French Revolution, or for plays such as *The Recruiting Officer* or *A Month in the Country*.

This pattern is for an over-the-knee version. You may also make them shorter or below the knee.

Fabric Suggestions

- Canvas, drill, denim, leather

Materials

- ½ yard fabric
- 2¼ yards ½-inch single fold bias tape
- 30 buttons, half inch
- ⅓ yard 1-inch elastic

Pattern Pieces

- Inside (cut 2)
- Outside front (cut 2)
- Outside back (cut 2)

Construction

- Following the instructions on page 3, enlarge pattern pieces and cut.
- Sew center front seams. Press open and topstitch ⅛ inch on either side of seam.
- Repeat with center back seams.
- Sew bias tape to top and bottom edges. Turn to inside and press. Topstitch in place.
- Fold back seam allowances on long straight sides. Mark buttonhole placement and stitch. (You could also use Velcro for the closure. Attach the soft side of the Velcro to the overlap and the stiff side to the underlap.)
- Attach buttons. Shank buttons work best with buttonholes, flat buttons as decoration with Velcro.
- Attach 4 inches of 1-inch elastic to bottom edges as indicated. This will hold the gaiter to the wearer's instep.

Note: This pattern could be bag-lined instead of bound (see spat pattern for instructions).

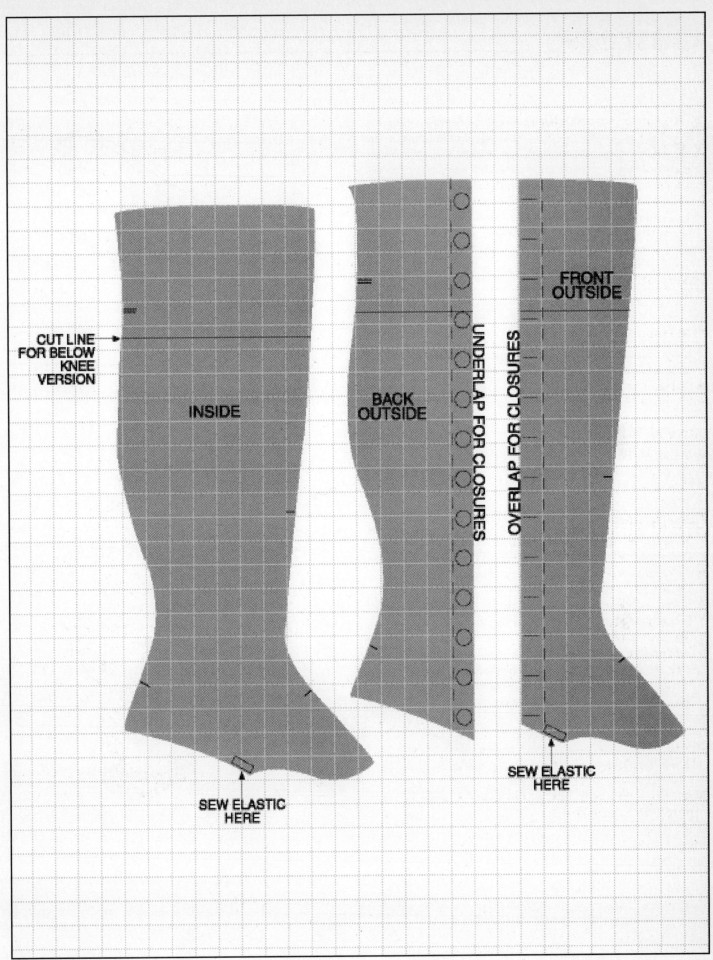

CUT LINE
FOR BELOW
KNEE
VERSION

INSIDE

BACK
OUTSIDE

UNDERLAP FOR CLOSURES

OVERLAP FOR CLOSURES

FRONT
OUTSIDE

SEW ELASTIC
HERE

SEW ELASTIC
HERE

Pattern is 25% actual size.

Slippers

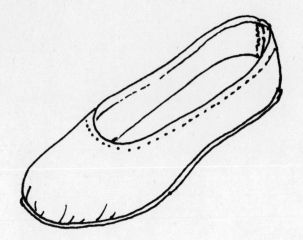

Slippers are lower than the ankle, and are usually without a means of fastening—they "slip" onto the foot. Slippers are usually worn indoors only. This pattern will make a nice Victorian "house slipper", or if made of leather would make a "ballet slipper" shaped shoe usable for the Renaissance period.

This pattern fits a man with a size 11 foot. For best results, trace the actor's foot while he is standing. For a custom sole pattern, add ¼-inch ease around the foot and smooth out the line to resemble the pattern given. Adjust upper to fit the custom sole and proceed as directed.

Fabric Suggestions

- Leather, upholstery tapestries, light weight carpeting

Material

- ½ yard fabric
- Dance rubber for sole
- 1½ yards ½-inch single fold bias tape

Pattern Pieces

- Upper slipper (cut 2—1 left and 1 right)
- Sole (cut 2—1 left and 1 right)

Construction

- Following the instructions on page 3, enlarge pattern pieces and cut.
- With right sides together, stitch heel seam. Press open and top-stitch seam allowance down. Sew bias tape around top edge of uppers. Turn to inside, press and topstitch in place.
- If you wish to attach a dance rubber bottom, cut out a set of soles from dance rubber without seam allowance. Place rubber on fabric sole pieces that include seam allowances. Center the rubber on the pieces. Stitch around rubber, close to the edge. Stitch around rubber one more time inside the previous stitch line. Proceed with attaching the sole to the slipper upper.
- Pin slipper upper to sole, matching centers and notches. Stitch. Turn right sides out.

Note: If you pre-wash and dry woven tapestry fabrics before making slippers you will get a nice "period" look and have excellent "give" for easing over the toe and heel areas.

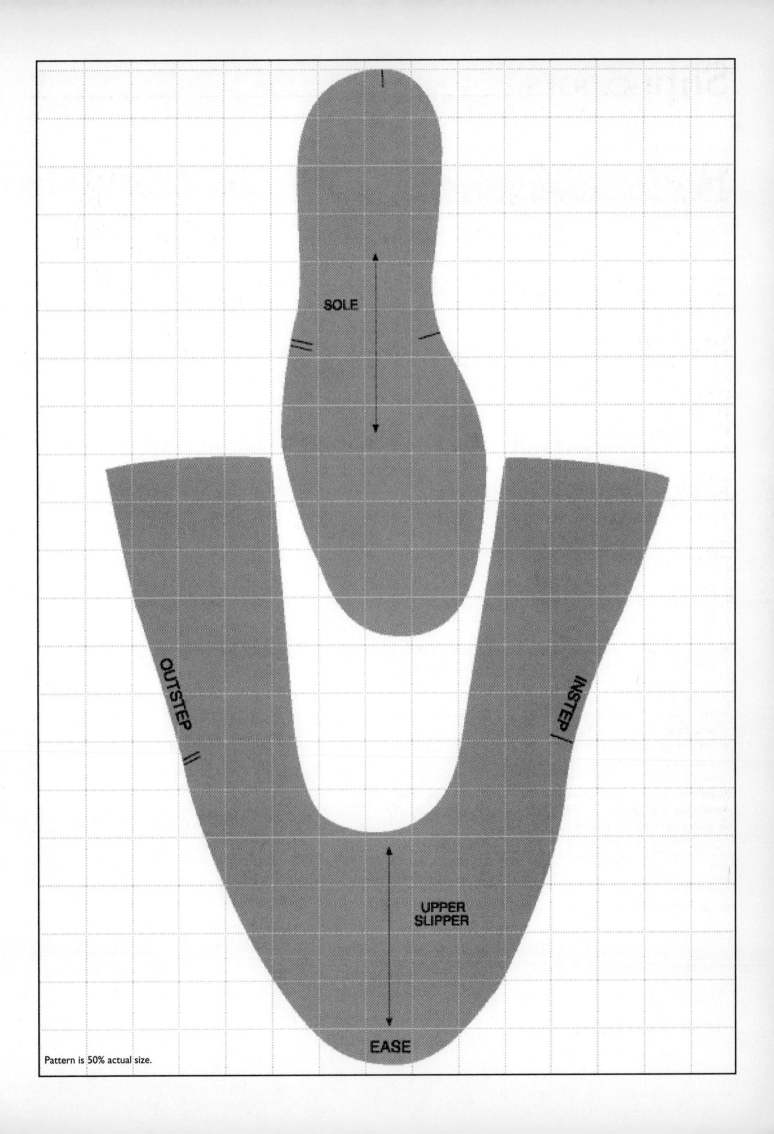

SOLE

EASE

OUTSTEP

INSTEP

UPPER
SLIPPER

EASE

Pattern is 50% actual size.

Soft Boots

Boots are, by definition, any shoe that extends above the ankle. This pattern makes a boot suitable for peasants in many periods, as well as a good general boot for anything set in the Medieval Period. They might be used in such plays as *The Lady's not For Burning, Becket, Macbeth*, or any of the morality plays.

This pattern fits a man with a size 10 foot. For best results, trace the actor's foot while he is standing. For a custom sole pattern, add ¼-inch ease around the foot and smooth out the line to resemble the pattern given. Adjust upper to fit the custom sole and proceed as directed.

Fabric Suggestions

- Lightweight leather, upholstery fabrics, ultrasuede

Materials

- ½ yard 60-inch goods
- Heavy weight fabric for sole
- Dance rubber if desired

Pattern Pieces

- Toe section (cut 2)
- Upper boot (cut 2)
- Sole (cut 2 fabric, cut 2 dance rubber without seam allowance if desired)

Construction

- Following the instructions on page 3, enlarge pattern pieces and cut.
- With right sides together, stitch toe section to upper boot, matching points A at center front of boot upper and center of top edge of toe piece. Clip curved seam and press. Topstitch if desired.
- With right sides together, stitch center back seam. Press. Topstitch if desired.
- If you wish to attach a dance rubber bottom, cut out a set of soles from dance rubber without seam allowance. Place rubber on fabric sole pieces that include seam allowances. Center the rubber on the pieces. Stitch around rubber, close to the edge. Stitch around rubber one more time inside the previous stitch line. Proceed with attaching the sole to the boot upper.
- With right sides together, stitch sole to upper boot. Turn right side out. Topstitch if desired.

Note: You could make the tops of the boots and hand sew them to a pair of purchased slippers.

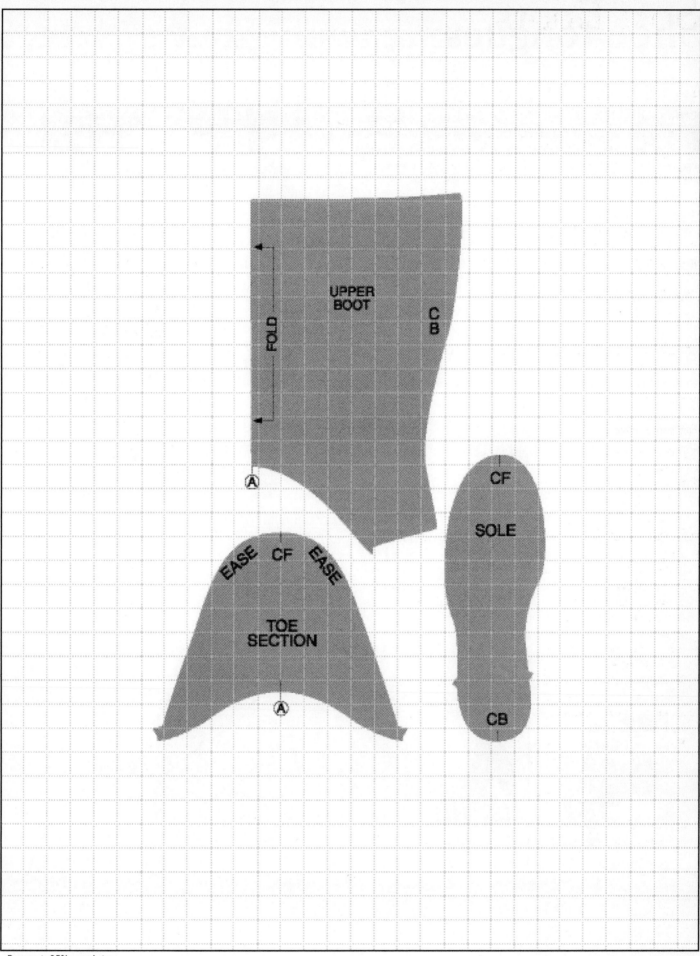

Pattern is 25% actual size.

Shoe tongues

From about 1620 to about 1790 shoes were made with high tongues, often extending far up the front of the shin. Unless you are having shoes custom-made for your production, you may wish to add a tongue to a modern shoe, to help achieve a period look. We have provided patterns for two sizes of tongues.

Fabric Suggestions

- Vinyl, leather, fabric to match shoe

Materials

- Small amount of leather or vinyl
- ⅓ yard ½-inch elastic
- Lining if desired

Note: If making tongues out of vinyl or other non-raveling materials, they need not be lined. However, if your are making them out of fabric to match a fabric shoe, they will need to be lined and interfaced.

Pattern Pieces

- Tongue (cut 4 fabric and 4 lining [if needed])

Construction

- Following the instructions on page 3, enlarge pattern pieces and cut.
- Stitch tongues together at center front. Repeat with lining.
- With right sides together, stitch linings to tongues leaving bottom edges open. Using pinking shears, trim seam allowances.
- Turn right sides out and press. Stitch bottom opening closed.
- Finishing: Tongues may be stitched directly to shoe or may be attached to a piece of elastic to slide over front of shoe. Trim as desired.

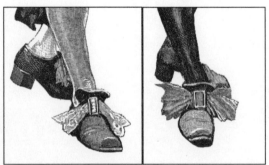

With Embellishment

Basic Shape

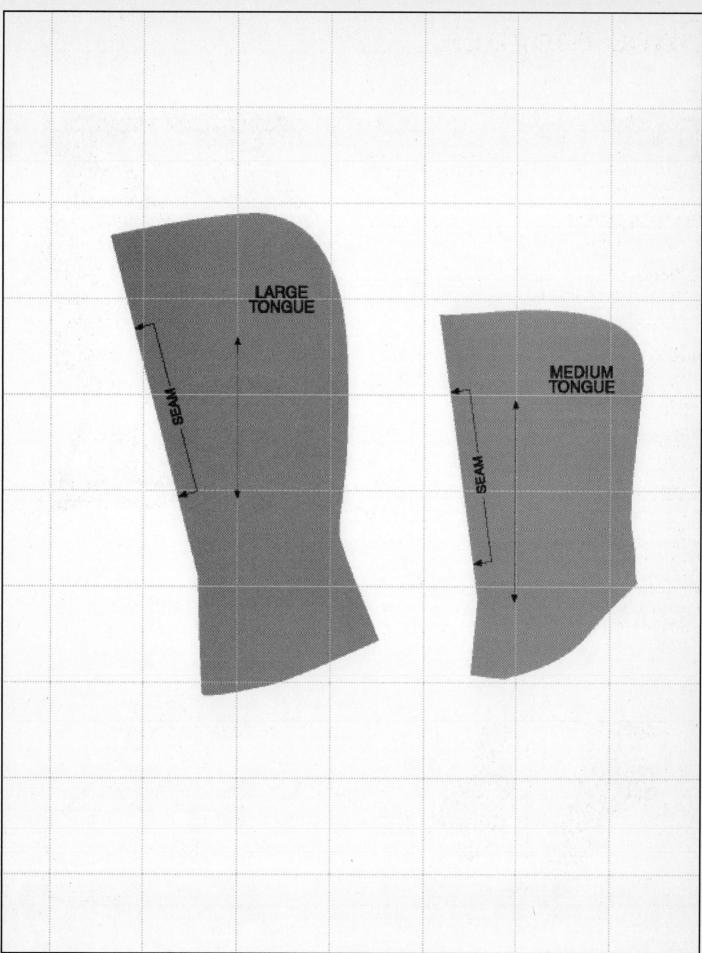

LARGE
TONGUE

SEAM

MEDIUM
TONGUE

SEAM

Chapter 5

BAGS & PURSES

Reticules

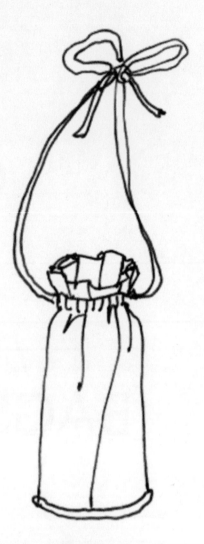

Reticules are small purses made of netting or lightweight fabric and usually closed with a drawstring. They were especially popular in the late 18th and early 19th centuries. Pockets were not made into clothing until the 20th century, and reticules allowed women to carry personal items with them. Often the reticule coordinated with a particular gown or ensemble and frequently featured beadwork or embroidery.

This reticule has a flat bottom; the shape is that of a miniature duffle bag.

Fabric Suggestions

- Light weight elegant fabrics such as dupioni silk, silk velvet, brocades

Materials

- ½ yard fabric
- ½ yard lining
- 1⅓ yards cording, satin rattail or ¼-inch ribbon
- Buckram, cardboard, or visor board

Pattern Pieces

- Body (cut 1 fabric and 1 lining)
- Bottom (cut 1 fabric, 1 lining, and 1 board without seam allowance)

Construction

- Following the instructions on page 3, enlarge pattern pieces and cut.
- Make buttonholes on the face fabric as indicated.
- With right sides together, stitch the side seam in fabric body. Repeat with lining.
- With right sides together, stitch lining and fabric together at top edge.
- Topstitch casing in place as indicated.
- Baste the two layers together at the bottom edge.
- Flat line the lining to bottom piece.
- With right sides together, stitch bottom edge of reticule to bottom piece. Press seam allowance toward top. Turn right side out and push board into place at bottom of reticule.
- Thread cording or ribbon through one buttonhole, around the bag, and out the same buttonhole. Knot the ends of the ribbon together. Repeat on other side. The two ribbons will cross each other inside the casing and will close the bag when pulled tight.

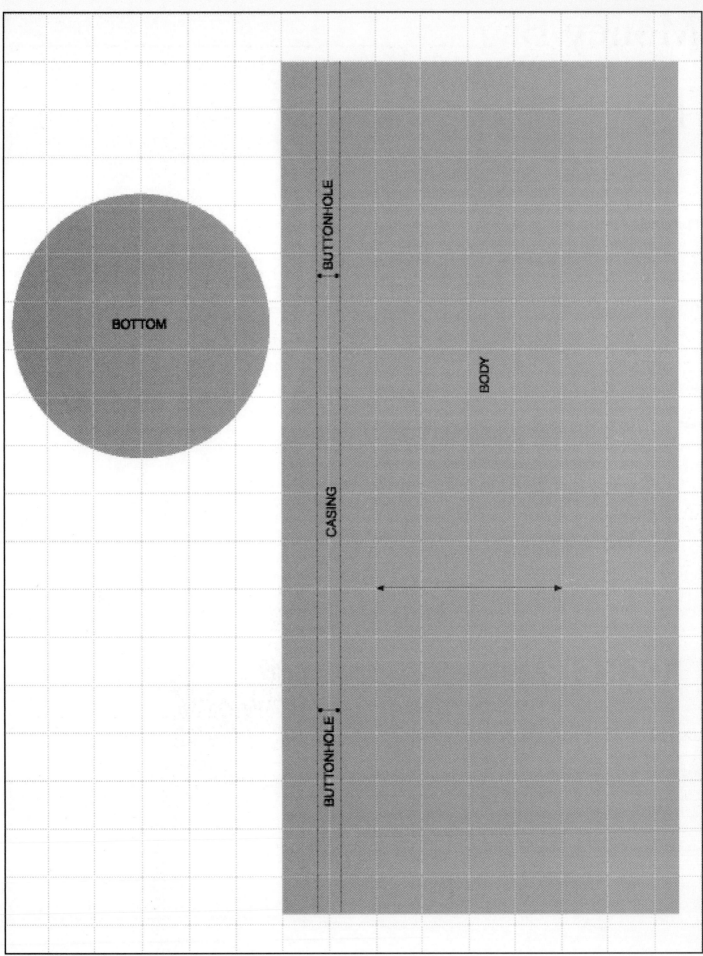

Pattern is 50% actual size.

Money Bag

This is a simple round drawstring bag. No production of *The Miser* would be complete without this costume prop. It also seems to be called for in a number of Shakespeare's plays. It could also be used for an 18th or 19th century reticule.

Fabric Suggestions

- Soft leather, velvet, brocade, soft tapestry, pleather, Ultrasuede

Materials

- ⅓ yard fabric
- ⅓ yard lining
- 1⅓ yards cording, satin rattail or ¼-inch ribbon

Pattern Pieces

- Bag (cut 1 fabric and 1 lining)

Construction

- Following the instructions on page 3, enlarge pattern piece and cut.
- Make buttonholes on the face fabric as indicated.
- With right sides together, stitch the lining and the face fabric together around outer edge leaving a place to turn. Clip curves, turn and press.
- Hand stitch opening closed.
- Topstitch casing in place where indicated.
- Thread cording or ribbon through one buttonhole, around the bag and out the same buttonhole. Knot the ends of the ribbon together. Repeat on other side. The two ribbons will cross each other inside the casing and will close the bag when pulled tight.

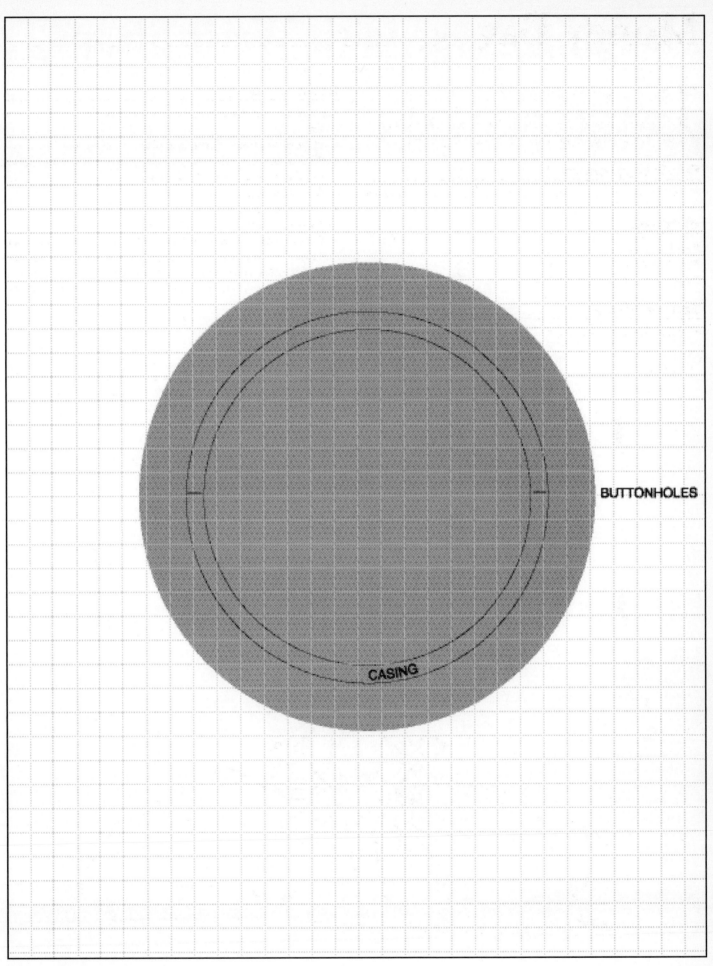

BUTTONHOLES

CASING

Pattern is 25% actual size.

Hanging Purse with Wrist Strap___

This small purse is another style of reticule. Popular during the 18th and 19th centuries, it hangs on the wrist and is open from the top.

Fabric Suggestions

• Satin, brocade, novelty embroidered fabrics

Materials

• ½ yard fabric
• ½ yard lining

Pattern Pieces

• Purse (cut 2 face fabric and 2 lining)

Construction

• Following the instructions on page 3, enlarge pattern piece and cut.

• With right sides together, stitch across the wrist end (the short straight side) of the purse. Repeat with lining.
• With right sides together, lay lining on top of purse, matching the wrist seam and all edges. Stitch the curved side openings. Clip the curves or trim the seam allowance with pinking shears. Turn right side out and press edges.
• Place right sides together, purse to purse and lining to lining, sandwiching the handle between the two layers. Stitch around the sides leaving a space open at the bottom of the lining and being careful not to catch the handle. Clip or pink the seam allowances. Turn right side out by turning the purse through the opening in the lining. Press the edges.
• Close the opening in the lining by hand sewing.
• Trim as desired.

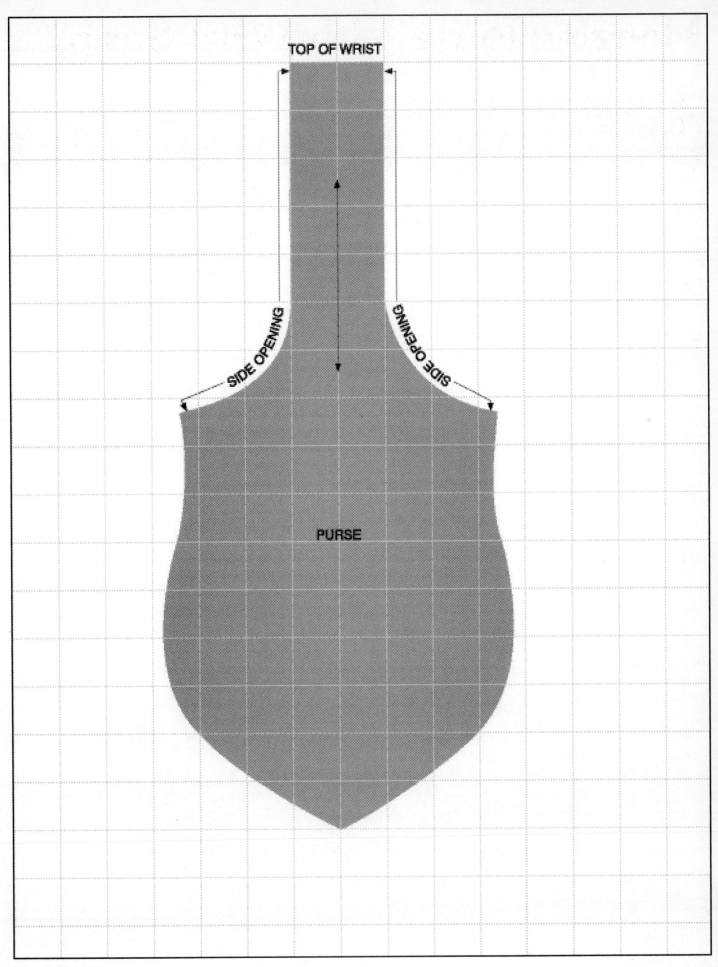

TOP OF WRIST

SIDE OPENING

SIDE OPENING

PURSE

Pattern is 50% actual size.

Miser's bag

A miser's bag hangs over the wrist and opens with a slit along the top edge. Contents are held in the 2 ends of the bag and secured with a sliding ring that closes the opening when in position. Popular during the 18th and 19th centuries, this type of purse was also know as a "stocking" purse. The word purse comes from the Greek word "byrsa" which means "to hide."

Fabric Suggestions

- Satin, brocade, novelty embroidered fabrics, knits.

Materials

- ¼ yard fabric
- ¼ yard lining
- 2 tassels
- 2 O rings, about 1" (larger if using thick fabric)

Pattern Pieces

- Purse (cut 1 fabric and 1 lining)

Construction

- Following the instructions on page 3, enlarge pattern piece and cut.
- Fold purse lengthwise with right sides together and stitch along the long seam, leaving the center open as indicated. Press seam open. Repeat with lining.
- Slide the lining piece into the fabric piece wrong sides together, making sure the openings are lined up. Hand stitch around the opening.

- Hand stitch a running stitch ½ inch from one of the raw end edges, being sure to go through both the face and the lining fabrics.
- Draw up the gathering thread and tuck the raw edges into the purse. Tie off the thread. Repeat with the other side.
- Stitch tassels onto each end.
- Slip the O rings onto the bag.

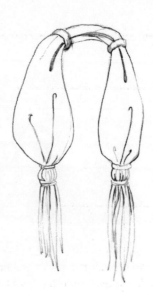

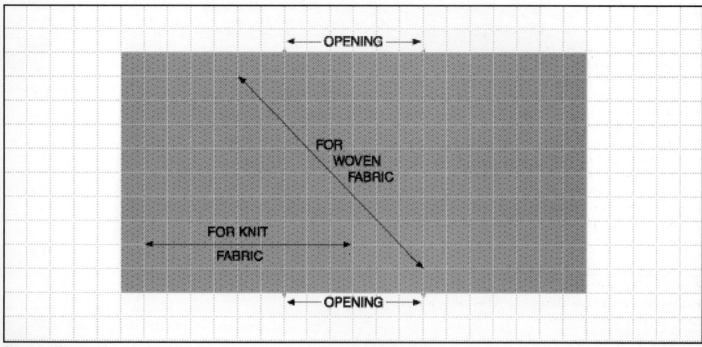

OPENING

FOR WOVEN FABRIC

FOR KNIT FABRIC

OPENING

Pattern is 25% actual size.

Saddle Bag

A connected pair of covered pouches, a saddle bag lies across the back of a horse behind the saddle. It could be taken off and worn over one shoulder by the rider. Appropriate for any play set in the "Wild West".

Fabric Suggestions

- Heavy woven fabric, leather, blanket fabric, canvas, drill, denim.

Material

- 1½ yard fabric

Pattern Pieces

- Base (cut 2)
- Facing (cut2)
- Pocket (cut 2)
- Gusset (cut2)
- Pocket flap (cut 4)

Construction

- Following the instructions on page 3, enlarge pattern pieces and cut.
- With right sides together, stitch outer edge of pocket to gusset. When machine stitching, place the gusset on bottom to allow for ease. Press seam allowances toward the gusset and topstitch.
- Hem top edge of pocket and gusset, finishing these pieces before sewing onto base.
- With right side together, sew shoulder seam of base. Press seam allowance open and topstitch.
- Sew right side of pocket to wrong side of base. Flip pocket right side out. Press seam allowance toward gusset and topstitch.
- With right sides together, pin facing to base. Stitch from pocket to pocket up over the shoulder on both sides. Clip curves and turn right side out. (There will be a small section that extends down into pocket.)
- Turn back seam allowance on each end of the facing and stitch in place inside the pocket.
- With right sides together, stitch 2 pocket flaps together around the curved side. Clip curves, turn right side out and press. Topstitch if desired. Repeat with other pocket flap.
- Place pocket flap on base above pocket, with raw edges extending into pocket. Stitch in place.
- Hook and loop tape, snaps or ties may be added to hold pocket flaps shut.

If using leather or a heavy non-raveling fabric, you may want to construct this with minimal seam allowances and stitch all seams together on the right side of the fabric. Edges can be bound or decoratively whip stitched if desired.

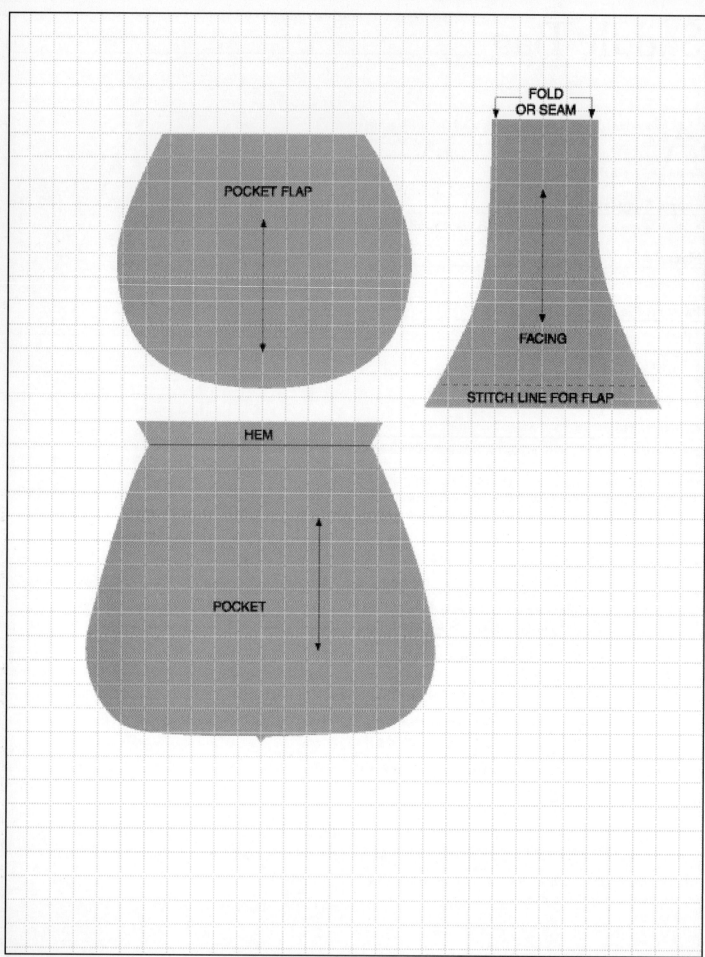

POCKET FLAP

FOLD
OR SEAM

FACING

STITCH LINE FOR FLAP

HEM

POCKET

Pattern is 25% actual size.

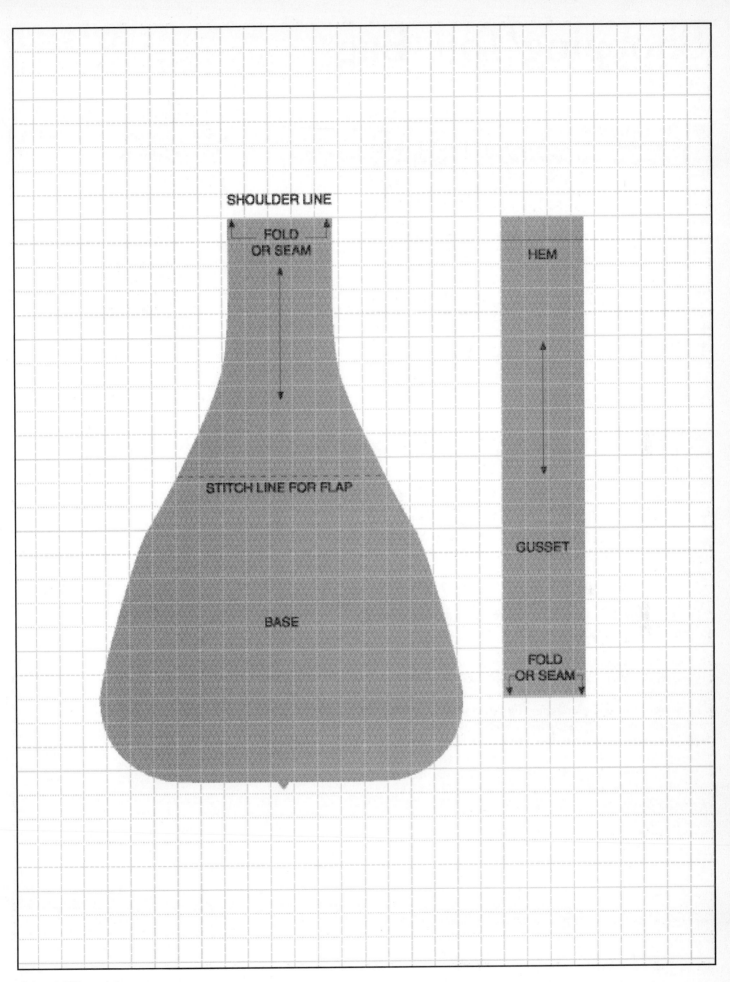

SHOULDER LINE

FOLD OR SEAM

HEM

STITCH LINE FOR FLAP

GUSSET

BASE

FOLD OR SEAM

Pattern is 25% actual size.

Shopping/Tote Bag

This pattern is for a roomy, flat-bottomed bag with an open top, suitable as a knitting bag, shopping bag, or diaper bag. You might find this pattern useful for productions of *Ten Little Indians* or any of the Miss Marple mysteries of Agatha Christie.

Fabric Suggestions

- Sturdy heavyweight fabrics, denim, drill, canvas, upholstery weight fabrics, quilted fabrics

Materials

- ½ yard fabric

Pattern Pieces

- Bag (cut 2)
- Handles (cut 2)
- Pocket (cut 1 or 2 as desired)

Construction

- Following the instructions on page 3, enlarge pattern pieces and cut.

Note: If you want to pockets on the inside or outside of bag, add them before constructing the bag.

- With right sides together, sew the sides and bottom edges of bag. (In order not to have a raw edge inside the bag, you may want to either sew a French seam, a flat felled seam or over-lock the raw edge.)
- At one of the corners, flatten out so the bottom seam lays on top of the side seam. Sew a line perpendicular to the bottom seam 3 inches from the corner, forming a triangle. Repeat with the other corner.
- Fold corner triangles back toward bottom seam and sew in place.
- Fold the top edge into bag ½ inch and press. Fold again 1 inch and press. Stitch top hem along first fold, ¾ inch from the top.
- With right sides together fold handle in half lengthwise and sew handle along the long edge. Turn right sides out and press. Topstitch along both long edges. Repeat with other handle.
- Fold raw edge of handle under and place onto bag where indicated. Stitch in a square and an X (see illustration). Making sure handle is not twisted, sew the other end of the strap to the bag where indicated.
- Repeat on the other side of the bag.

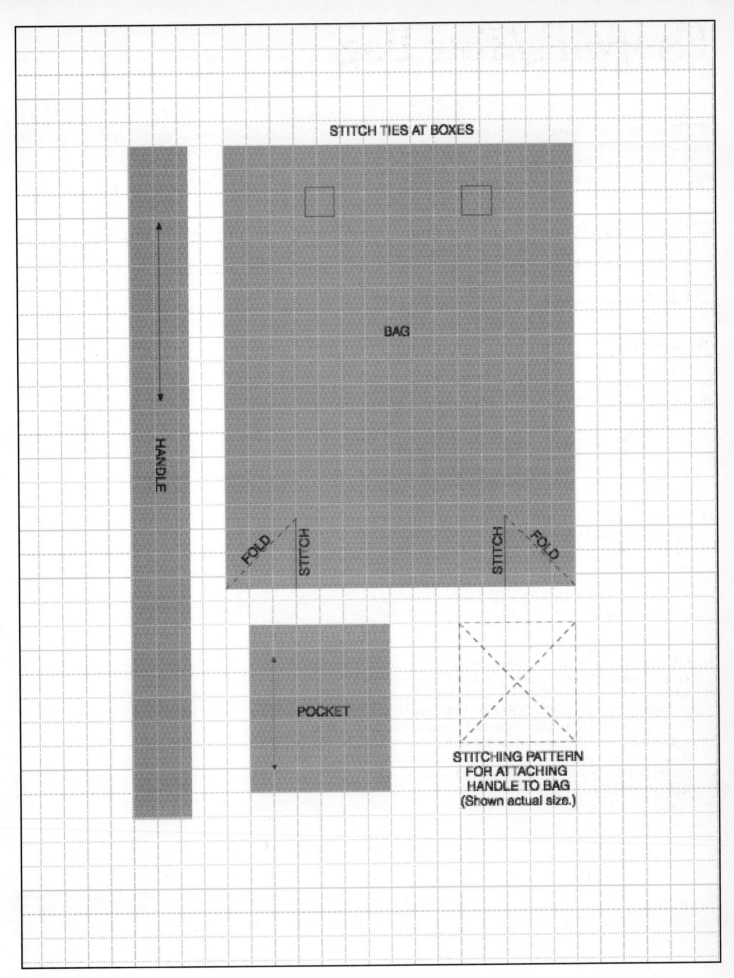

STITCH TIES AT BOXES

HANDLE

BAG

FOLD STITCH

STITCH FOLD

POCKET

STITCHING PATTERN
FOR ATTACHING
HANDLE TO BAG
(Shown actual size.)

Pattern is 25% actual size.

Duffle Bag

A sturdy cylindrical bag originally carried by sailors and other military personnel, duffle bags can be used in productions of *Anna Christie*, *On the Town*, and *South Pacific*. This pattern also makes a great laundry bag.

Fabric Suggestions

- Denim, drill, canvas

Materials

- 1½ yards 54"- 60" wide fabric or 2 yards 36"- 48" wide fabric
- 3 yards cording
- 4 grommets; inside diameter larger than the cording
- 1 yard webbing, 1½ inches wide (for handle if desired)

Pattern Pieces

- Body (cut 1)
- Base (cut 1)

Construction

- Following the instructions on page 3, enlarge pattern pieces and cut.

- Place grommets (or a large buttonholes) as indicated for the drawstring.
- With right sides together, stitch the side seam of body stopping 1" short of the seam allowance at the top edge.
- Topstitch seam allowances down side of bag.
- With right sides together, stitch the body of the duffle bag to the base. Clip curved seam allowance. Press seam allowance toward body. Topstitch through body and allowances.
- Fold under seam allowance at top edge of bag. Fold over again to form casing. Topstitch into position.
- Thread the cord through the casing starting at one of the grommets and coming out the second grommet on the same side. Knot the two ends together. Repeat on other side. The two cords will cross each other to form two ties that will close the bag when pulled up.

Note: If you wish to add a handle to the side of the bag, it is best to do so before sewing up the side seam. Lay a length of cotton canvas belting down into the desired position and stitch each end securely to form a handle.

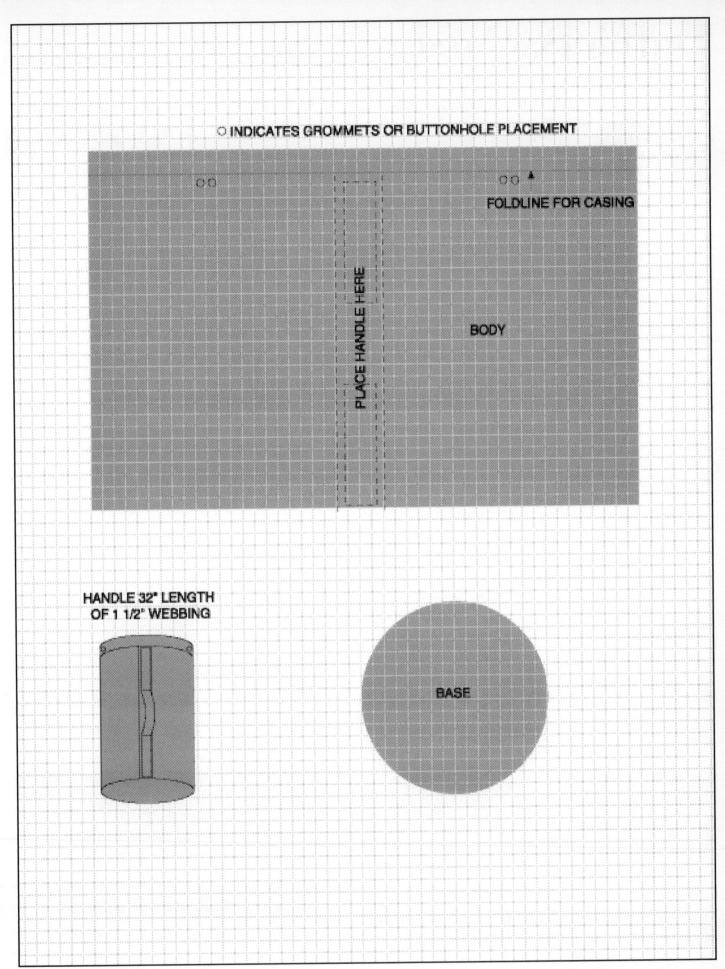

○ INDICATES GROMMETS OR BUTTONHOLE PLACEMENT

FOLDLINE FOR CASING

PLACE HANDLE HERE

BODY

HANDLE 32" LENGTH
OF 1 1/2" WEBBING

BASE

Pattern is 1/8th actual size.

Envelope Purse

This handbag is so named because of its envelope shape. It was very popular in the 1930s and 1940s—in the 1940s they were often quite large and were carried in the crook of the arm. This would be a great accessory for productions of *The Women*, *The Cradle Will Rock*, or any stylish play of the period.

Fabric Suggestions

- Sturdy fabrics such as brocades, leather, or tapestry fabrics. Thinner fabrics that match the costume may be used if they are bonded for stability.

Materials

- ⅜ yard fabric
- ⅜ yard lining

Pattern Pieces

- Purse (cut 1 fabric and 1 lining)

Construction

- Following the instructions on page 3, enlarge pattern piece and cut.
- With right sides together, fold handbag along bottom fold line. Stitch along the side seams in the face fabric, being careful not to proceed into the inside edge seam allowance.
- Repeat with lining.
- With right sides together, sew lining to face fabric around flap, and from fold line to fold line. Clip corners, turn and press.
- Turn flap right sides out and put lining to the inside of purse.
- Turn seam allowances in along the inside edge and hand stitch closed.
- Attach snap or button as indicated.

Costume sketch by Robin L. McGee for "Rosie" in *Bye Bye Birdie*.

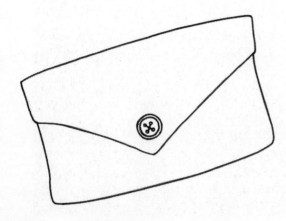

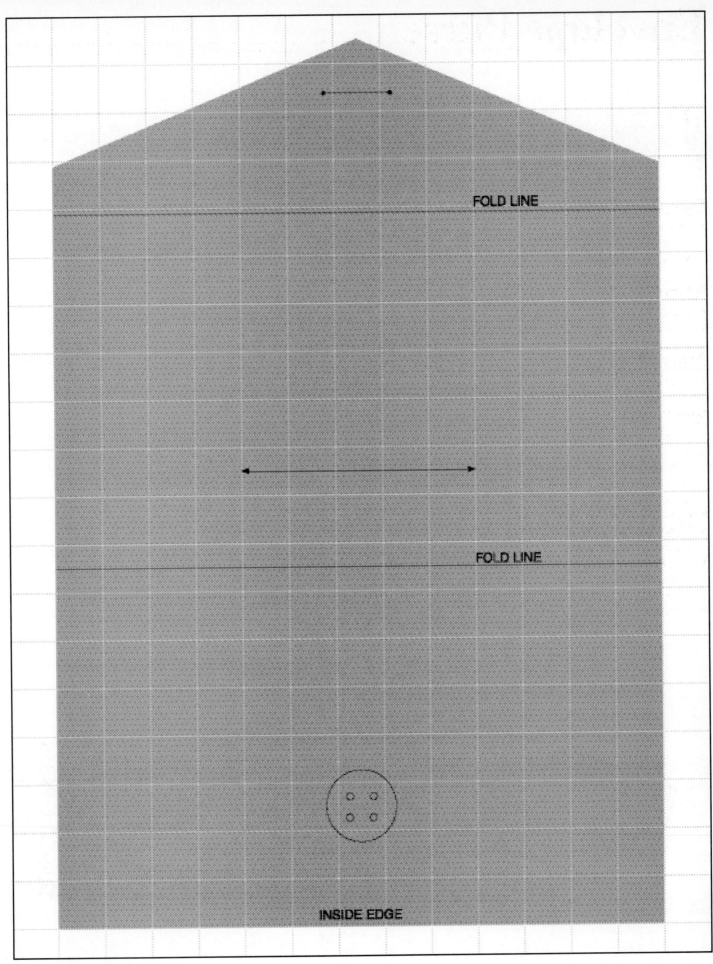

FOLD LINE

FOLD LINE

INSIDE EDGE

Pattern is 50% actual size.

Pockets

Originally, a "pocket" was a separate garment, usually hanging from the waist and used to carry money and small personal effects. The fashion began in the Elizabethan era when men hung them from their belts. In the 1700s women wore them under their panniers and skirts, leading to the eventual placement of pockets into garments.

Fabric Suggestions

- Decorative satins and brocades if the pocket is to be seen.

Materials

- ½ yard fabric
- 2 yards ½-inch double fold bias binding

Pattern Pieces

- Pocket (cut 1 front and 1 back)

Construction

- Following the instructions on page 3, enlarge pattern piece and cut.
- Cut slit into front of the pocket as indicated. Bind the edges of the slit with bias binding.
- Lay pocket front onto pocket back, wrong sides together. Stitch around pocket close to the edges. Bind outside edge of pocket.
- Bind top edge of pocket, adding ties if desired, or attach to garment when appropriate.

Reproduction pocket by Sarah K. Havener.

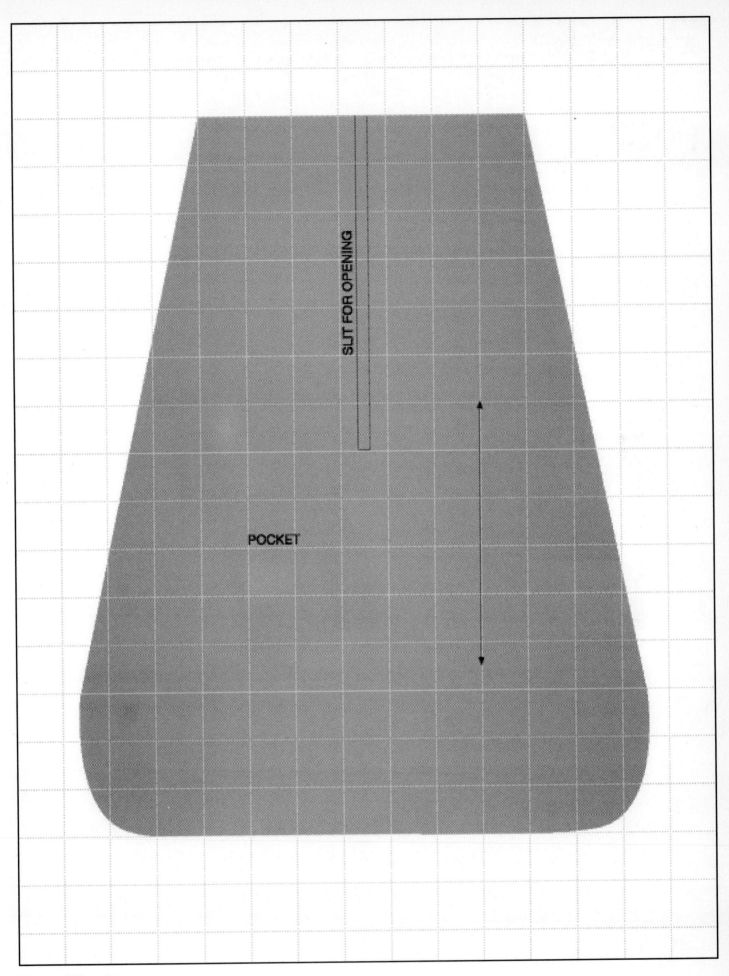

SLIT FOR OPENING

POCKET

Pattern is 50% actual size.

Chapter 6

HANDWEAR

Gloves

Sheaths for each finger distinguish a glove from a mitt or a mitten. Gloves with separate fingers first appear in the 12th century—they were cut as two pieces and seamed together. A separate piece for the thumb developed later. In the 1700s, white gloves came to be considered the most elegant and were worn for formal occasions. This practice has continued into the 21st century.

Fabric Suggestions

- Leather (kid, pig chamois, or suede) ultrasuede, lightweight satin, lace, lightweight stretch fabrics

Materials

- ½ yard fabric

Pattern Pieces

- Body (cut 4)
- Forchette #1 (cut 2)
- Forchette #2 (cut 2)
- Forchette #3 (cut 2)
- Thumb (cut 4)

Construction

- Following the instructions on page 3, enlarge pattern pieces.
- Lay the actor's hand on the enlarged pattern for the glove body and make any adjustments as needed. Cut, making sure you have a right- and a left-handed glove. We suggest 1/4 inch seam allowance. If making gloves from woven, non-stretch fabric, cut the glove on the bias as indicated. If using stretch fabric, cut the pieces so the maximum amount of stretch goes around the hand.
- With right sides together, sew around the top and the side of the thumb.
- With right sides together, sew the thumb piece to the glove matching points A to A and B to B.
- Sew the forchettes to the thumb side of the glove body between each finger as indicated. Forchette number 1 is placed between the index and middle finger. Forchette number 2 is placed between the middle finger and the ring finger. Forchette number 3 is placed between the ring finger and the pinky finger.
- Sew the front of the glove to the back of the glove along the sides and around each finger following the forchettes you have just sewn in place.
- Repeat with the other glove.
- Hem the bottom edges of the gloves. Trim as desired.

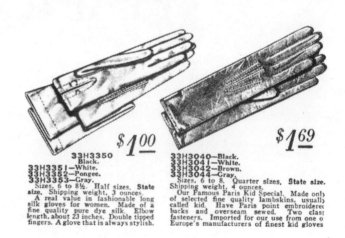

$1⁰⁰

33H3350
Black.
33H3351—White.
33H3352—Pongee.
33H3353—Gray.
Sizes, 6 to 8½. Half sizes. State size. Shipping weight, 3 ounces.
A real value in fashionable long silk gloves for women. Made of a fine quality pure dye silk. Elbow length, about 23 inches. Double tipped fingers. A glove that is always stylish.

$1⁶⁹

33H3040—Black.
33H3041—White.
33H3042—Brown.
33H3044—Gray.
Sizes, 6 to 8. Quarter sizes. State size. Shipping weight, 4 ounces.
Our Famous Paris Kid Special. Made only of selected fine quality lambskins, usually called kid. Have Paris point embroidered backs and overseam sewed. Two clasp fasteners. Imported for our use from one of Europe's manufacturers of finest kid gloves

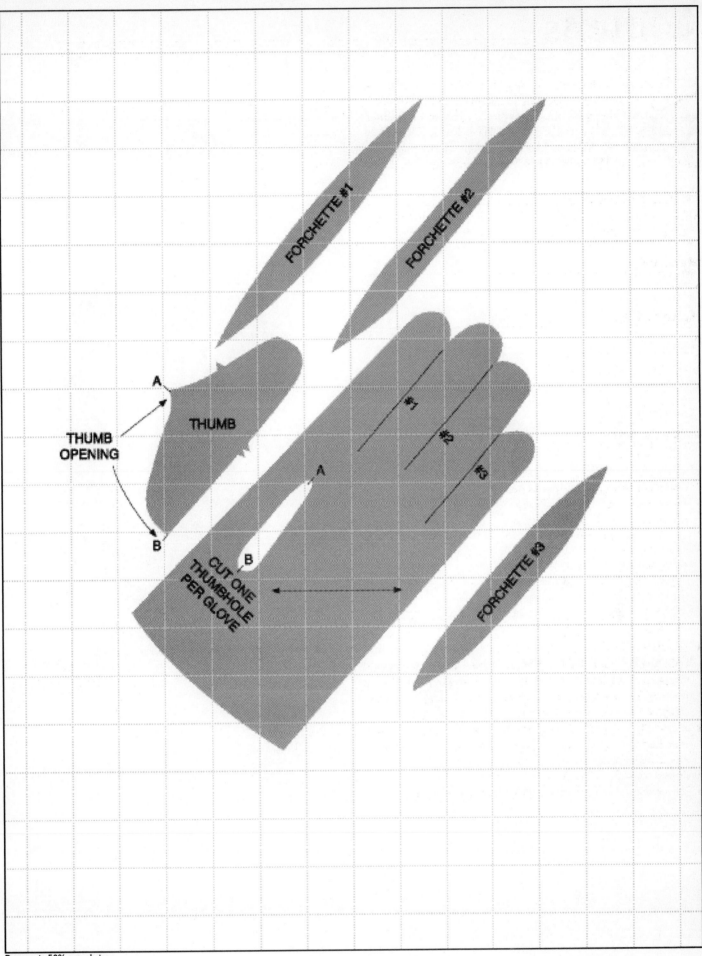

Pattern is 50% actual size.

Mittens

Often worn for warmth in winter, mittens are a covering for the hand and wrist with a section for all four fingers and a separate section for the thumb. Mittens would be appropriate for any play set during the winter months such as, *Meet Me in St. Louis* or *Little Women*.

This pattern is based on a pair of 1940s mittens.

Fabric Suggestions

- Wool, polar fleece, fake fur

Materials

- ½ yard fabric
- ⅔ yard fabric ¼-inch elastic

Pattern Pieces

- Body (cut 2)
- Thumb (cut 2)

Construction

- Following the instructions on page 3, enlarge pattern pieces and cut.
- Sew an easing stitch around the top of the thumb. Gently gather/ease.
- Fold the thumb section that is attached to the body up to the wrong side of the mitten. With right sides together, sew thumb to body starting at point A, around top of the thumb and down the palm of the mitten. Turn thumb right side out.
- Fold the body, bringing right sides together. Sew from point A down to the hem edge. Moving the thumb out of the way, sew from point A around the top of the mitten.
- Cut elastic into two 9-inch long pieces. Sew edges of each piece together to form a circle.
- Stretch and zigzag elastic to line as indicated on pattern.
- Turn up bottom edge of mitten and hem.

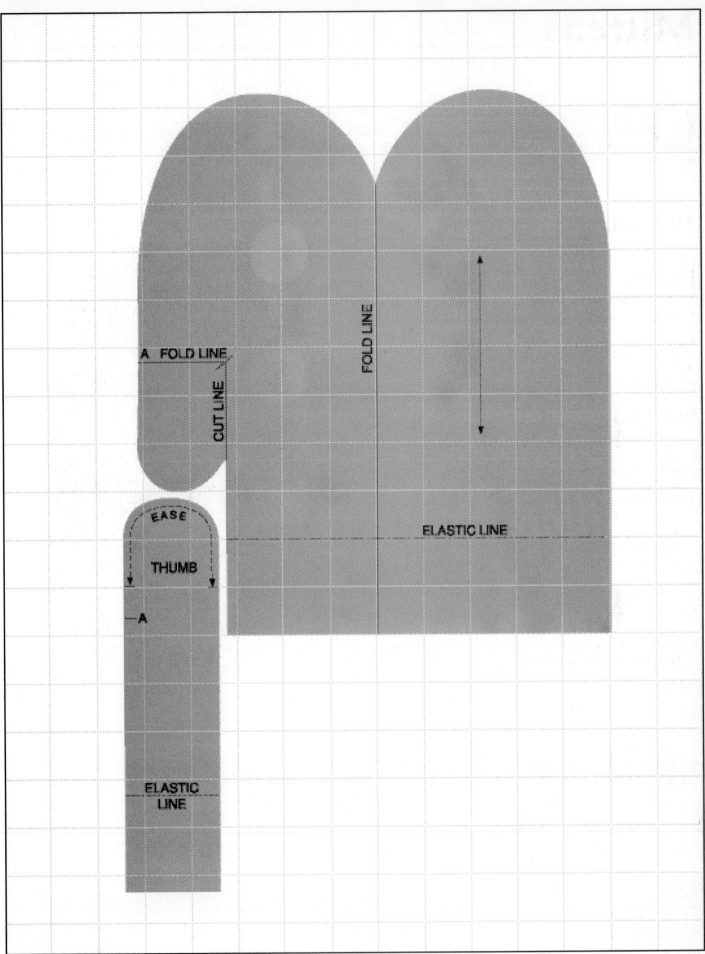

A FOLD LINE

CUT LINE

FOLD LINE

EASE

THUMB

A

ELASTIC LINE

ELASTIC
LINE

Pattern is 50% actual size.

Mitts

itts are fingerless gloves. Popular in colonial America, they offered warmth but did not get in the way while doing chores. Mitts are now often worn for weddings or other formal occasions. We offer patterns for thumbed and chapel mitts.

Fabric Suggestions

• Any stretch fabric

Materials

• ⅔ yard fabric

Pattern Pieces

• Chapel Mitt (cut 2)
• Thumbed Mitt (cut 4)

Construction

• Following the instructions on page 3, enlarge pattern pieces and cut.

Thumbed Mitt

• With right sides together, sew side seams and seams between thumb and finger openings. Use a stretch stitch or small zigzag to allow for stretch.
• Carefully hemstitch around the thumb hole, finger opening and top of mitt.

Chapel Mitt

• With right sides together, sew side seam on each mitt as indicated. Use a stretch stitch or small zigzag to allow for the stretch.
• Turn up hems on both ends of the mitt and stitch.
• Hand stitch a small elastic loop to the point of the mitt to slip over the middle finger.

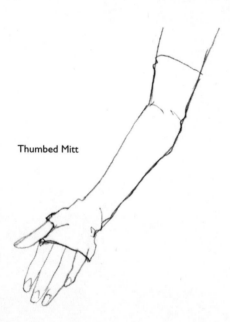

Thumbed Mitt

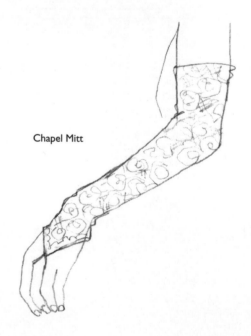

Chapel Mitt

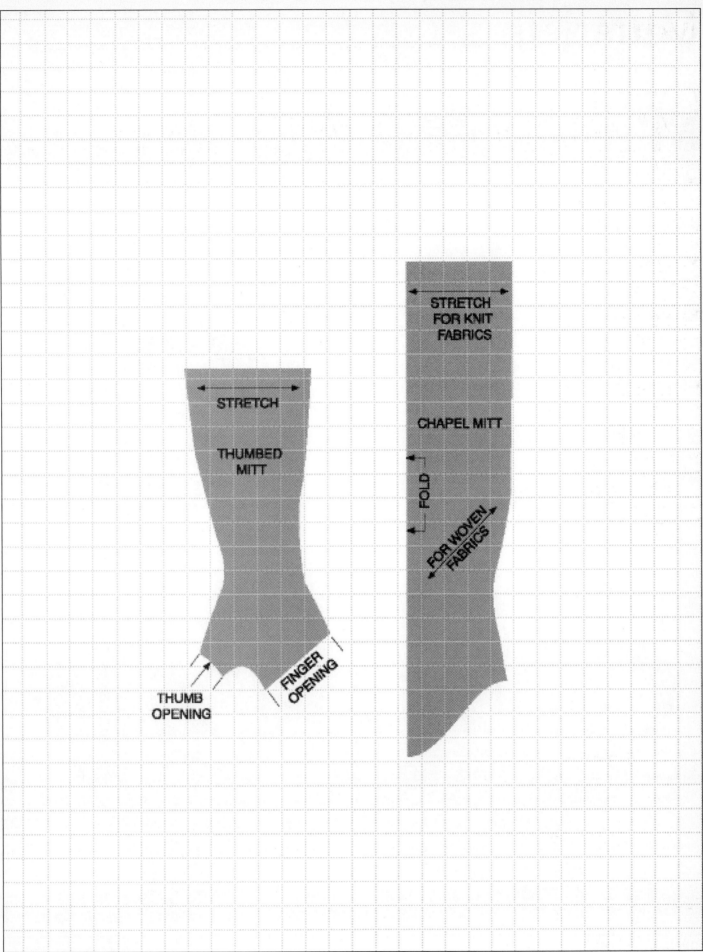

STRETCH

THUMBED
MITT

THUMB
OPENING

FINGER
OPENING

STRETCH
FOR KNIT
FABRICS

CHAPEL MITT

FOLD

FOR WOVEN
FABRICS

Patterns are 25% actual size.

Gauntlets

Originally a glove with a portion that extended to cover part of the arm, gauntlets later became separate garments. The phrase "take up the gauntlet" is to accept a challenge. The phrase "throw down the gauntlet" is to issue a challenge.

Fabric Suggestions

- Leather, suede, upholstery fabric, denim, vinyl

Materials

- ¼ yard fabric
- 1 pair gloves
- fringe or trim as desired

Pattern Pieces

- Gauntlet (cut 2 fabric and 2 lining if needed)

Construction

- Following the instructions on page 3, enlarge pattern piece and cut.
- With right sides together, sew the side seam. Repeat with lining.
- With right sides together, stitch fabric and lining together at top of cuff. Turn right sides out and press. Topstitch if desired.
- Sew any desired trim at this point.
- Turn cuff inside out and place glove inside it, right sides together. Place the side seam of the gauntlet at the "pinky" side of glove. Stitch. Flip gauntlet up.

Notes: If you are making these out of leather you will not need a lining. You may wish to inset fringe into the side seam before sewing.

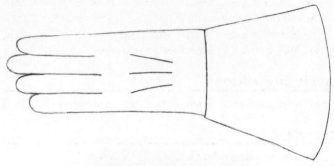

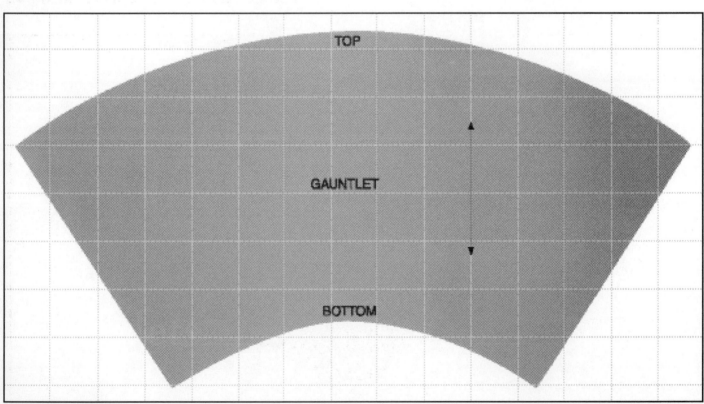

TOP

GAUNTLET

BOTTOM

Pattern is 50% actual size.

Pilgrim/Cavalier Cuff _____

A standing cuff that flares out as it extends up from the wrist, as the name suggests it was in style during the 16th and 17th centuries. These cuffs may be unadorned or extremely lavish, and they were usually attached to over garments rather than being part of a shirt or chemise. Use these cuffs in such plays as *The Crucible*, *The Devils* or for a Thanksgiving pageant.

Fabric Suggestions

- Sturdy woven fabrics; linen, cotton, wool gabardine

Materials

- ½ yard fabric (¼ yard for face, ¼ yard for lining)

Pattern Pieces

- cuff (cut 2 fabric, 2 lining)

Construction

- Following the instructions on page 3, enlarge pattern piece and cut.
- With right sides together, sew the side seam. Repeat with lining.
- With right sides together, stitch the face fabric and the lining together at the top of cuff. Turn right sides out and press. Top-stitch if desired.
- Sew any desired trim at this point.
- Turn up seam allowance of bottom edge to inside of cuff. Slip-stitch closed.

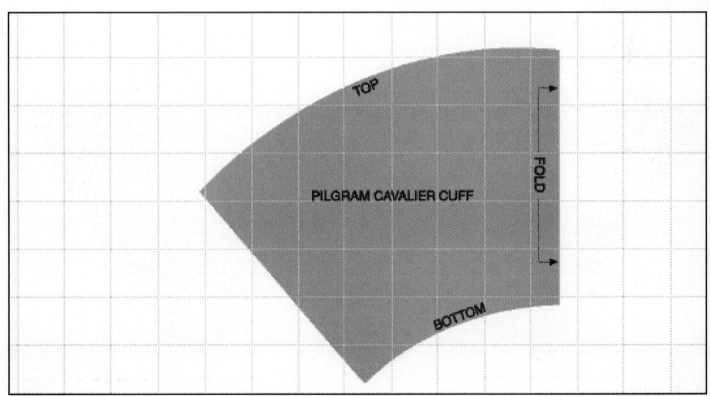

TOP

FOLD

PILGRAM CAVALIER CUFF

BOTTOM

Pattern is 50% actual size.

French Cuff

A lthough most often seen attached to the sleeve of a shirt, women waitresses in Playboy Clubs (a.k.a. bunnies) wore French cuffs without a shirt. This pattern does not fold back on itself and is fastened with cufflinks.

Fabric Suggestions

- Stiff shirt weight cotton, linen, or blend

Material

- ¼ yard medium weight woven
- ¼ yard interfacing
- Cuff links

Pattern Pieces

- Cuff (cut 4 fabric, 2 interfacing)

Construction

- Following the instructions on page 3, enlarge pattern piece and cut.
- Attach interfacing to wrong side of fabric.
- With right sides together, sew two cuff pieces together leaving a 3-inch space at wrist to turn. Clip corners and curves, turn, and press.
- Slipstitch the opening closed.
- Topstitch, if desired.
- Make buttonholes as indicated.
- Wear with cufflinks.

Costume sketch by Robin L. McGee for dancers on "The Friars Club Roast of Jerry Stiller" on Comedy Central.

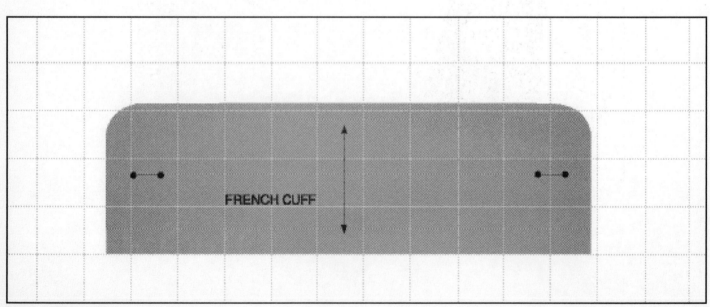

FRENCH CUFF

Pattern is 50% actual size.

Large Flat Muff

This large muff was popular during the Victorian era and would be appropriate for any drama by Dickens, such as *A Christmas Carol*. In extravagant form these could be carried by men in Restoration comedies such as *The Way of the World* or *The School for Scandal*.

Fabric Suggestions

- Fur, fake fur, satin, velvets, marabou boa for "Feather Muff"

Materials

- ½ yard face fabric
- ½ yard lining
- ½ yard batting

Pattern Pieces

- Muff, 16" × 28" (no pattern given: cut 1 fabric, 1 lining, and 1 batting)

Construction

- Cut all layers as indicated above.
- Lay fabric pieces on table as follows: Fabric face up, lining face down over fabric, then batting over lining. Pin together and stitch along 28" sides through all 3 layers.
- Turn right sides out, so that the right side of the fabric is on one side and the right side of the lining is on the other with the batting in between the two.
- Fold in half, bringing the right sides of the fabric together, lining up the raw edges. (The lining will be on the outside.)
- Pin the batting and the face fabric layers together; do not include the lining. Stitch along raw edges, through fabric and batting.
- Turn raw edges of lining under and hand stitch the lining closed.
- Turn muff right side out.
- Stitch hanging loop on one side if desired. Decorate as desired.

Note: To make a "Feather" muff, follow all directions and then stitch rows of marabou onto face of muff in parallel rows about 2½ inches apart.

Small Round Muff

A muff is a cylindrical shaped object covered with fur or other material into which the hands are placed from either end to keep them warm. The word muff comes from the Medieval Latin word "muffula" which means "glove." This style was extremely popular during the early 1800s. This accessory might be used in a production of *A Christmas Carol*.

Fabric Suggestions

- Velvet, fur, fake fur, satin, damask

Materials

- ½ yard face fabric
- ½ yard lining
- high-loft batting
- ⅔ yard ½-inch single-fold bias binding
- 16 inches ⅞-inch (#5) ribbon for wrist loop

Pattern Pieces

- Muff (cut 1 fabric, 1 lining, 1 batting)

Construction

- Following the instructions on page 3, enlarge pattern piece and cut.
- Mark all darts on the lining fabric. Stitch darts into the wrong side of the lining. Press darts in one direction.
- With right sides together, stitch seam in the lining, making a tube with darts at the ends. Press seam open.
- Lay the batting over the lining with the wrong side facing the batting. Baste or pad stitch the batting to the lining, taking long stitches on the batting side and small "pick" stitches on the lining side.

- Mark the darts on the wrong side of the fabric face. Pin a small pleat where each dart is marked. These pleats will line up with the darts in the lining. Stitch across the pleats at the seam line to hold in position.
- With right sides together, stitch the seam (the non-pleated sides).
- Lay face fabric right side out over lined batting, matching seam allowances and seam of muff to seam of lining.
- Bind edges using bias tape or self-bias.
- Hand stitch hanging loop to one side of muff at seam, if desired.

FIGURE 13 H
(Costume 6479)

FIGURE 14 H
(Jacket 6480)
(Skirt 6495)

DELINEATOR   DESCRIBED ON PAGE 35   JANUARY, 1903
25

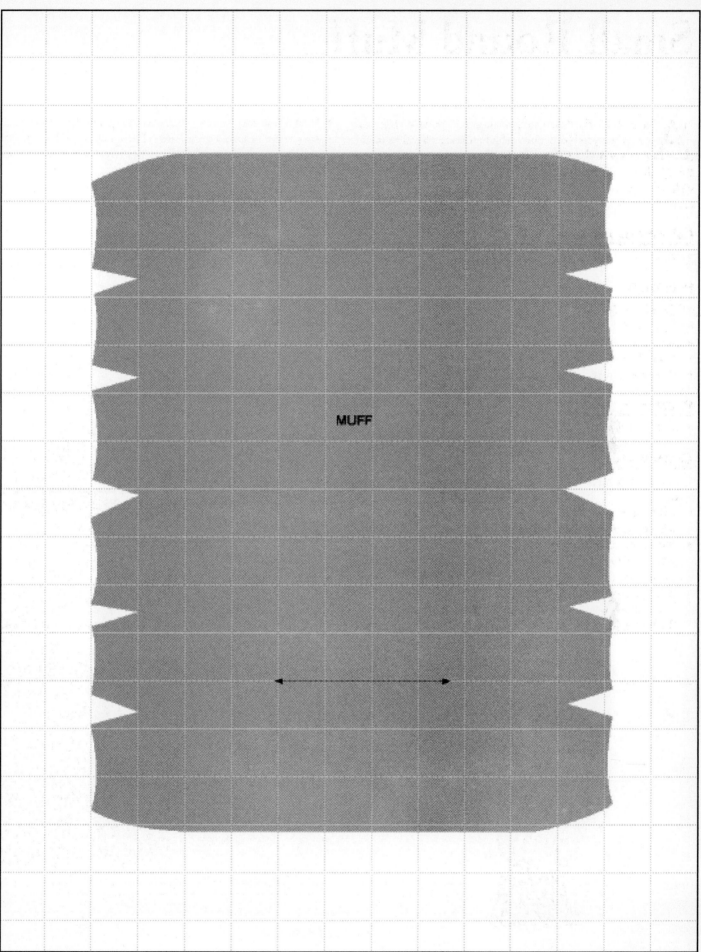

MUFF

Pattern is 50% actual size.

Chapter 7

MISCELLANEOUS PATTERNS

Handkerchiefs

Small, usually square pieces of cloth used for personal purposes (such as blowing a nose) or as clothing accessories, at various times handkerchiefs were a required accessory for the upper classes. They were often perfumed to mask the unpleasant odors of common life. How the handkerchief was used and/or carried were all parts of the social hierarchy. Handkerchiefs were also part of the social order of mourning in Victorian England, changing color, size, and style as the level of mourning dictated. During 17th and 18th century England a woman returning to church after the birth of a child made an offering of a white handkerchief.

Fabric Suggestions

- Light weight wovens, cotton, silk, linen

Construction

- Cut a square of fabric the desired size plus seam allowances.
- Hem and/or trim the four sides.

Standard sizes

- Modern man's handkerchief 12-16 inches
- Modern woman's handkerchief 10-15 inches
- Bandana/ neckerchief 23 inches

Pocket Square

A square of silk, often matching the tie, a pocket square is worn in the upper left breast pocket of a man's suit or formalwear. The fashion began when men placed their handkerchief into the pocket; later it developed into a distinct style.

Fabric Suggestions

- Any soft decorative fabric, charmeuse silk

Materials

- ½ yard fabric

Construction

- Cut a square 16 inches
- Hem all sides
- Decoratively fold and insert in breast pocket of suit or sports coat.

Fake Pocket Squares

This is a theatrical version of the pocket square, attached to a card to insure proper wear by the actor.

Fabric Suggestions

- Silk brocade, foulard, tie fabric, satin

Materials

- Card stock
- ¼ yard fabric

Construction

- Cut a piece of card stock 4 inches by 5 inches.
- Cut two 3-inch squares of fabric.
- Fold the squares in half forming a triangle, then fold again. (All the raw edges should be together now.)
- Place triangles on card stock and stitch in place.

Variations

#2

- Cut one 4 inch square and two 2 inch squares.
- Fold as above and attach.

#3

- Cut a rectangle 4 inches by 9 inches.
- Fold short edges back ½ inch.
- Fold in half lengthwise.
- Fold in half widthwise.
- Stitch in place.

#1

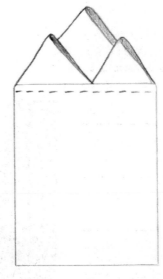

#2

#3

Epaulettes

The word literally means "small shoulder," in French; from épaule "shoulder." Originated as a device to hold a shoulder belt or bandoleer in place, it evolved into an ornate shoulder badge worn by military officers to indicate rank. Often the width and length of the trim and fringe on the epaulette directly correspond to the wearer's rank, regiment, or branch of service. We have included two shapes to choose from.

Fabric Suggestions

- Uniform wool or twill

Materials

- ¼ yard fabric
- cardboard, buckram, or visor board
- batting
- 1¼ yard piping or edging
- ⅔ yard fringe
- ¼ yard non-raveling fabric for backing (such as felt or suede-cloth)
- 2 snaps
- 2 large hooks and bars

Pattern Pieces

- Epaulette (cut 2 fabric with seam allowance, 2 backing without seam allowance, and 2 boards with out seam allowance)

Construction

- Following the instructions on page 3, enlarge pattern piece and cut.
- Remember to cut base with no seam allowance out of the visor board, cardboard or buckram. Cut two, remembering to reverse for a left and a right. (If you are using buckram, you will need to wire the edges for stability.)
- Glue a layer of batting over top of base pieces.
- Lay top fabric over base (padded side against the wrong side of face fabric). Clip seam allowance as needed and glue to back of epaulette base.
- Stitch or glue on piping or other trimmings as desired.
- Cut out backings for epaulettes without seam allowances.
- Stitch hook and snap to epaulette backing as indicated on the pattern.
- Glue backing to bottom side of epaulette base covering all raw edges of cover fabric and trims.
- Pin fringe to rounded section of epaulette. Stitch in place.
- Stitch the other half of snap and the bar for the hook onto the garment.

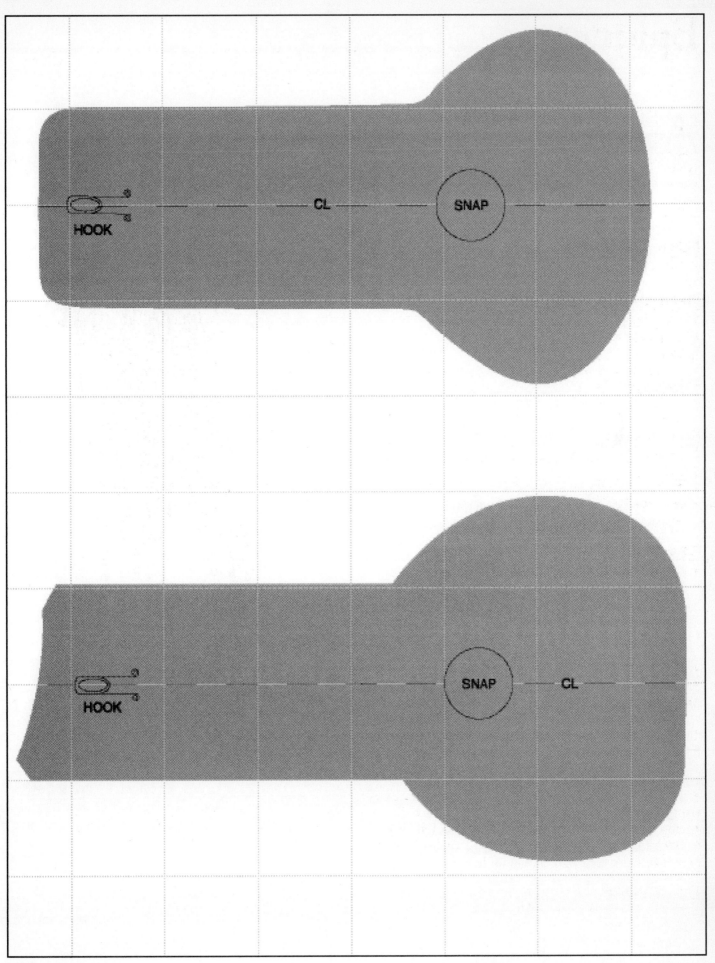

Patterns are actual size.

Baldric

A baldric or bandoleer is a belt, band, or sash worn diagonally across the body, originally to support a sword or a bugle. They are often worn by the military or royalty to signify rank. During the Restoration, baldrics were a part of fashionable dress and did not signify military rank or royalty. Plays that might use a baldric are *The Recruiting Officer*, or any of the plays of Moliere or Congreve.

Fabric Suggestions

- Satins, brocades, faille, leather

Materials

- ½ yard fabric
- ½ yard interfacing
- ½ yard lining

Pattern Pieces

- Front and back (cut 2 fabric, 2 interfacing, 2 lining)

Construction

- Following the instructions on page 3, enlarge pattern piece and cut.
- Attach interfacing to wrong side of fabric.
- With right sides together, sew the front to the back at the shoulder seam. Press seam open. Repeat with lining.
- With right sides together, sew face fabric to lining, leaving bottom open to turn.
- Turn right sides out. Press.
- Trim as desired.
- At the bottom edges, press seam allowance up into opening and hand stitch closed.
- Place front piece on top of back piece as indicated and stitch in place.

Variation

Bandolero Style

- Following the instructions on page 3, enlarge pattern piece and cut.
- With right sides together, sew the front to the back at the shoulder seam. Press seam open. Repeat with the lining.
- With right sides together, sew face fabric to lining along the side seams, leaving bottom open to turn.
- Turn right sides out and press.
- With right sides of the face fabric together stitch the bottom point closed being careful not to catch the lining
- Fold back the seam allowance in the lining and hand stitch closed.
- Trim as desired.

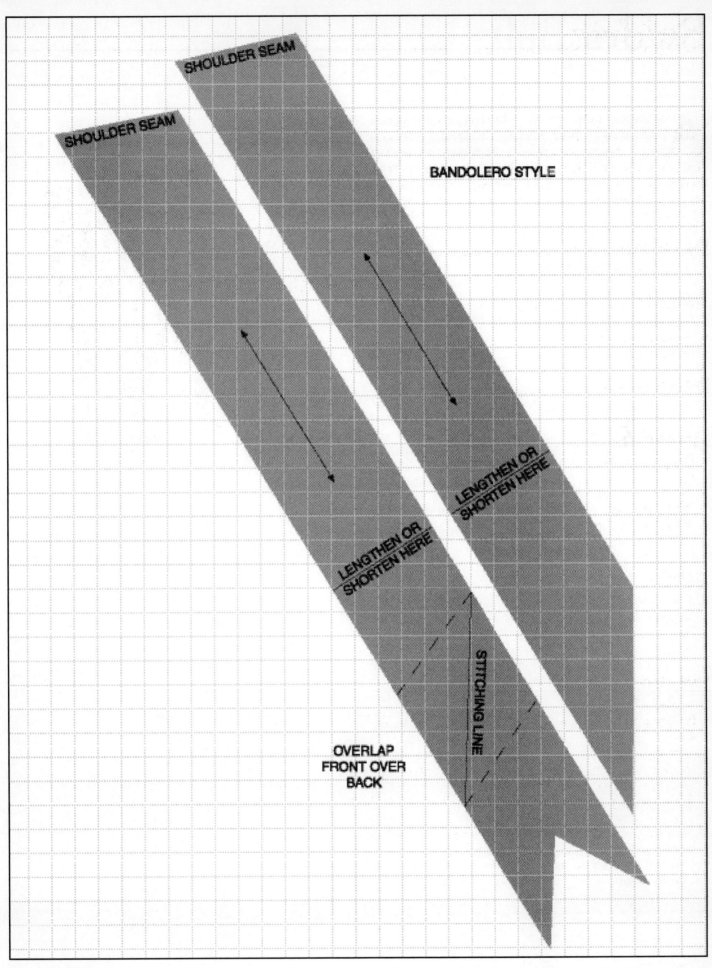

SHOULDER SEAM

SHOULDER SEAM

BANDOLERO STYLE

LENGTHEN OR
SHORTEN HERE

LENGTHEN OR
SHORTEN HERE

STITCHING LINE

OVERLAP
FRONT OVER
BACK

Pattern is 25% actual size.

Sword Belt

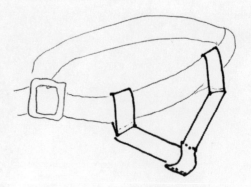

A sword belt is simply an extension, hanging from the belt or shoulder, from which a sword could be hung. The sword belt is sometimes considered a costume and sometimes considered a prop. If you can make a sword belt instead of relying on the prop people, you can have one that will match the costume, but make sure to coordinate with them as to the size and kind of the sword.

This pattern is a very rough guideline for a regular sword. If you're using a broad sword, you will need to make all the pieces wider to accommodate the weight and breadth of the sword.

Fabric Suggestions

- Webbing, leather, heavy bullion trim, or upholstery trim

Pattern Pieces

- *Belt carriers:* (cut 2). The length will be the width of the belt (from which you intend to hang sword) times two, plus seam allowances. (If cutting out of leather, the desired width of the carriers is usually around 1½ inches for a sword that will be used for onstage battle.)
- *Front piece:* (cut 1). The length will be the distance from the belt to just below where the actor wants to grab the sword handle, usually around 6½ inches, but this will vary with the actor's height and arm length.
- *Back piece:* (cut 1). The length will be about 11 inches long (again, this will vary with the actor's size) plus about 3 inches for fold-over and stitching.

Construction

- Stitch the front piece of the sword belt to the forward end of the back piece at stitch line A. They should overlap each other at an angle of about 120 degrees. Push the back piece on top of the front so that the back piece is arched and lines up with stitch line B. This creates the space where the sword will be carried. Paper clip or baste these lines.
- For a fitting, tape the sword hanger (front and back) to the carriers. With the sword and the actor, figure the correct angle for the belt carriers and the hanging unit to be attached. Stitch the carriers and hanging unit together. Slip the belt through the carriers.
- This sword belt attaches to a waist or hip belt. It can be a purchased Garrison belt, work belt, or any style that is appropriate for the costume and the period.

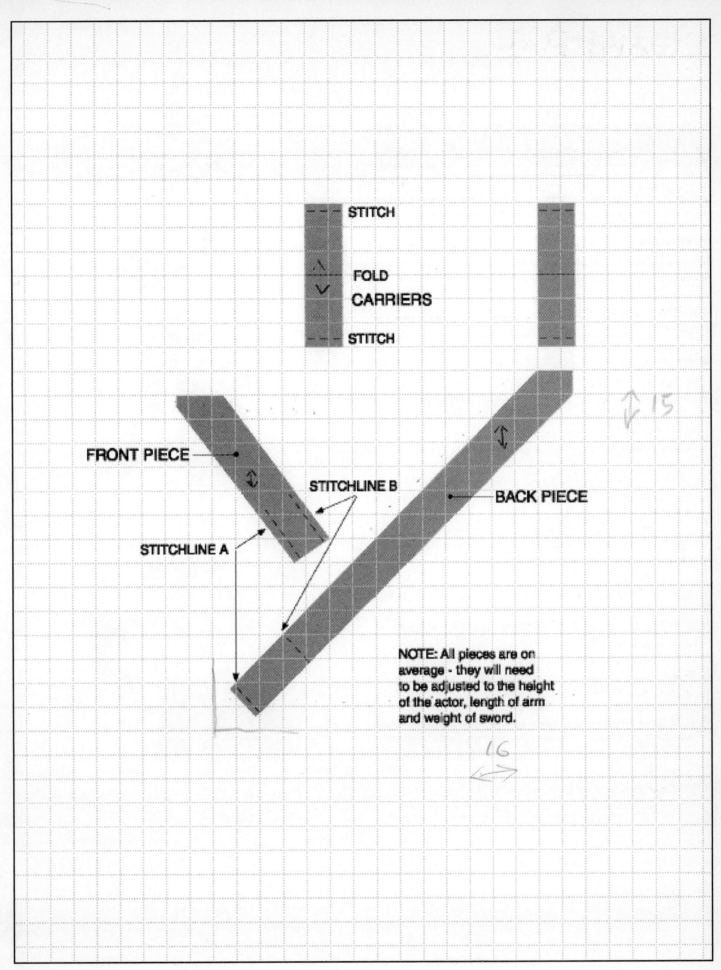

STITCH

FOLD

CARRIERS

STITCH

FRONT PIECE

STITCHLINE B

BACK PIECE

STITCHLINE A

NOTE: All pieces are on average - they will need to be adjusted to the height of the actor, length of arm and weight of sword.

Pattern is 25% actual size.

Quiver

A Quiver is a case for holding arrows. This simple tubular variation with a shoulder strap is perfect for your production of *Robin Hood*, or for a Valentine's Day Cupid.

Fabric Suggestions

- Vinyl, leather, ultrasuede, heavy canvas

Materials

- 1 yard material or 1 skin
- 6 inch square of cardboard
- 17 inches of feather boning, Rigilene, or wire

Pattern Pieces

- Quiver (cut 1)
- Base (cut 1 of material with seam allowance, 1 of cardboard with no seam allowance)
- Shoulder strap (cut 1 40 inches by 1½ inches finished)

Construction

- Following the instructions on page 3, enlarge pattern pieces and cut.
- If the shoulder strap is being made out of a fabric that ravels, fold in half lengthwise and stitch the long seam. Turn right side out.
- Lay the quiver down, right side up. Pin the shoulder strap where indicated, being sure to tuck in the raw edges of the two ends. Stitch in place.
- With right sides together, stitch the side seam of the quiver. Press the seam allowance to one side and glue down or top-stitch.
- With right sides together sew the base to the bottom end of quiver. Turn right side out.
- Slide cardboard base into quiver and push it snuggly against the bottom.
- Curl the feather boning, Rigilene, or wire into a circle to fit inside top opening.
- Fold the top edge of the quiver over the boning, Rigilene, or wire. Stitch in place, enclosing the boning—this will keep the top of the quiver open so that the arrows do not get stuck.

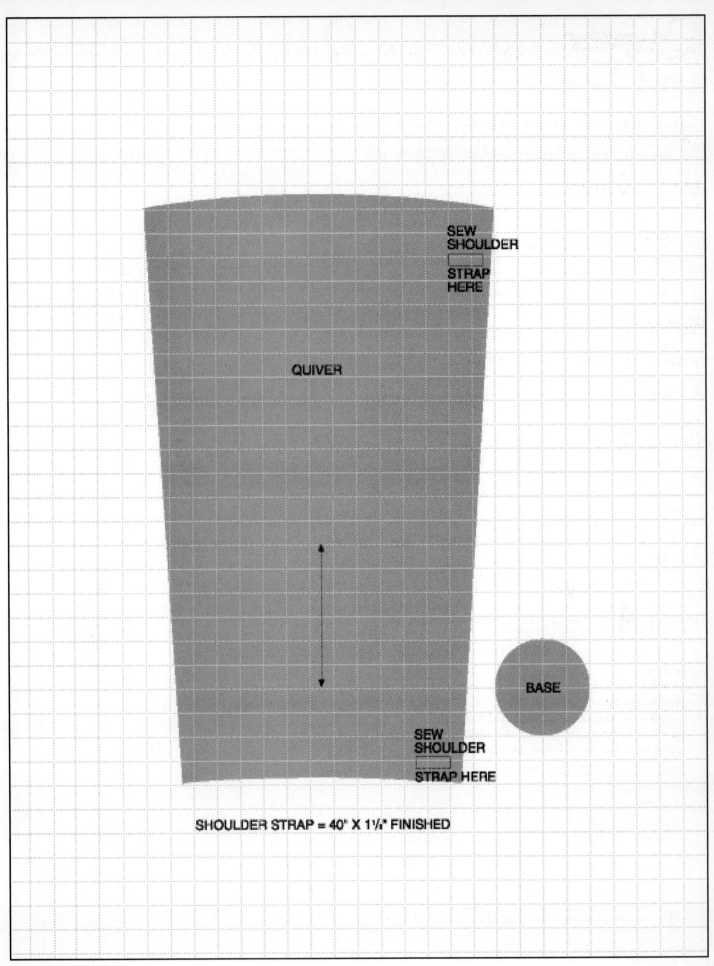

SEW
SHOULDER
STRAP
HERE

QUIVER

BASE

SEW
SHOULDER
STRAP HERE

SHOULDER STRAP = 40" X 1¼" FINISHED

Pattern is 25% actual size.

Native American Quiver and Bow Case

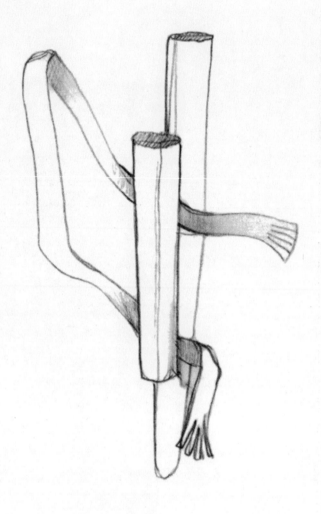

This is a case for holding arrows and a bow. The style is Native American, derived from a Plains Indian method of construction. The quiver and bow case would have been made from elk or buffalo hide. It is most authentic when made using the irregular shapes and textures found in leather.

Fabric Suggestions

- Leather, suede, ultrasuede, vinyl, canvas

Materials

- 1 yard material or 1 skin
- 2-foot long piece of dowel, or a straight stick
- Leather lacing, fake sinew, or heavy-weight thread

Pattern Pieces

- Quiver (cut 1)
- Base (cut 1)
- Bow case (cut 1)
- Shoulder strap (cut 1, 3" wide × actor's height)

Construction

- Following the instructions on page 3, enlarge pattern pieces and cut.

Quiver

- Lay quiver flat on table. Punch holes as indicated on pattern. Loosely thread leather lacing, fake sinew, or heavy thread through the holes. Leave the lacings loose for now.
- With right sides together, stitch side seam of quiver. Press seam allowance to one side and glue down.
- Sew base to quiver at the narrow end. Turn right side out.

Bow Case

- Lay bow case flat on table. Punch holes as indicated on pattern. Loosely thread leather lacing, fake sinew, or heavy thread through the holes. Leave the lacings loose for now.
- Fold the bow case pattern piece in half lengthwise; stitch down the side seam and around the bottom curve. Clip curve, press seam allowances to one side, and glue down.

Shoulder strap

- Fringe the last 3 inches at each end of strap. Piece or patch the leather if necessary to achieve the desired length.
- Lay the quiver on a flat surface. Put the shoulder strap ends over the quiver, matching a line 8-inches from the end of the strap, along the lacing line as indicated on pattern. Lay the bow case on top. Slide the dowel or stick down the sides of the quiver and bow case, going in and out of the lacings. Pull the lacings snug, so that the quiver, bow case, and shoulder strap are all held together.
- Decorate as desired.

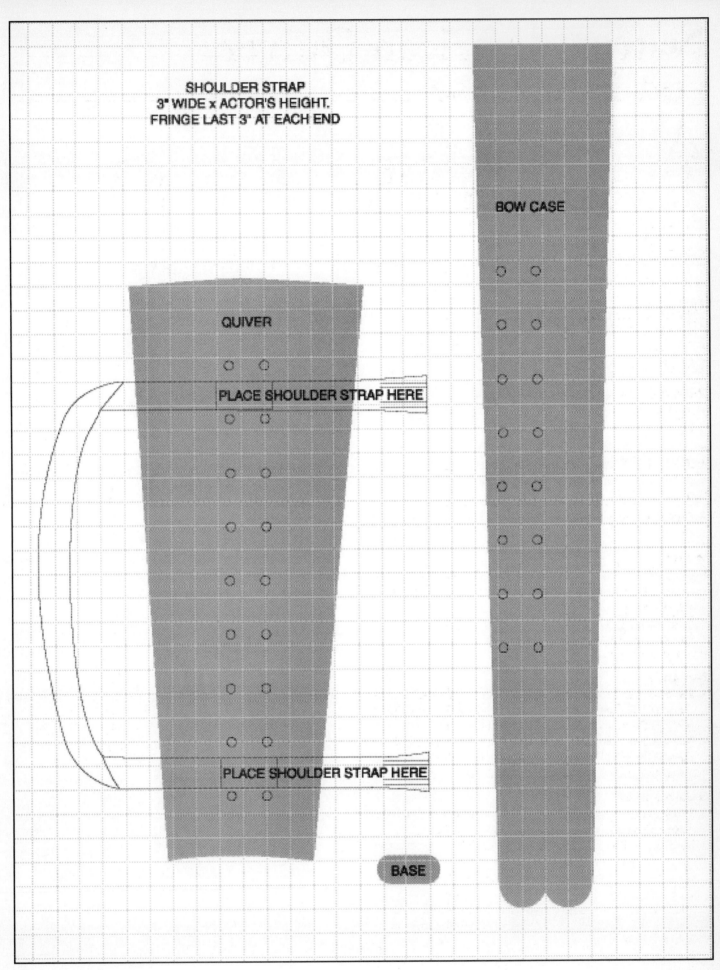

SHOULDER STRAP
3" WIDE x ACTOR'S HEIGHT.
FRINGE LAST 3" AT EACH END

BOW CASE

QUIVER

PLACE SHOULDER STRAP HERE

PLACE SHOULDER STRAP HERE

BASE

Pattern is 25% actual size.

Scabbard

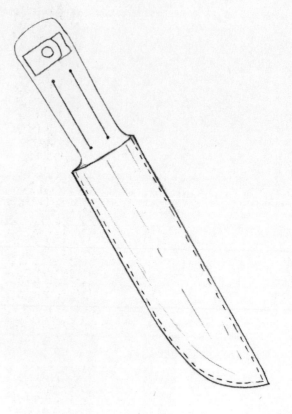

A scabbard is a sheath for a sword, dagger, or bayonet. Since each knife that you may be using for a production could be different, follow our directions but make a scabbard to fit your specific knife. Scabbards may be plain leather or be highly decorated. The choice will be based on the production and the character. (The word Scabbard can also be used to describe the case for an umbrella.)

Fabric Suggestions

- Leather (best), heavy vinyl, bonded ultrasuede

Materials

- Leather or other material (about 1 square foot)
- Snap

Pattern Pieces

- Scabbard base (cut 1)
- Knife sheath (cut1)
- Strip of leather for closure

Construction

- To make the pattern, trace around the blade and handle of the knife, indicating where the blade joins the handle.
- Add seam allowance—the seam allowance around the blade should be ⅜ inch deep, and the seam allowance around the handle should be ⅛ inch deep. Be sure the blade sheath does not taper in toward the handle, or the blade may not fit in the scabbard. This is your base. Cut 1 from the join of the handle down to the point. This will be the top of the knife sheath.
- Lay the knife sheath onto the base, right sides up. Stitch around knife sheath leaving the top edge open.
- Cut 2 vertical slits on the base, above the knife sheath, through which to pass a belt.
- Cut a strip of leather about ½ inch wide. Stitch this leather strip about ½ inch down from the top of the base. Slide the knife into the sheath and wrap this band around the handle. Mark an overlap the width of a snap to hold the knife in the scabbard.
- Stitch on or machine set a snap.

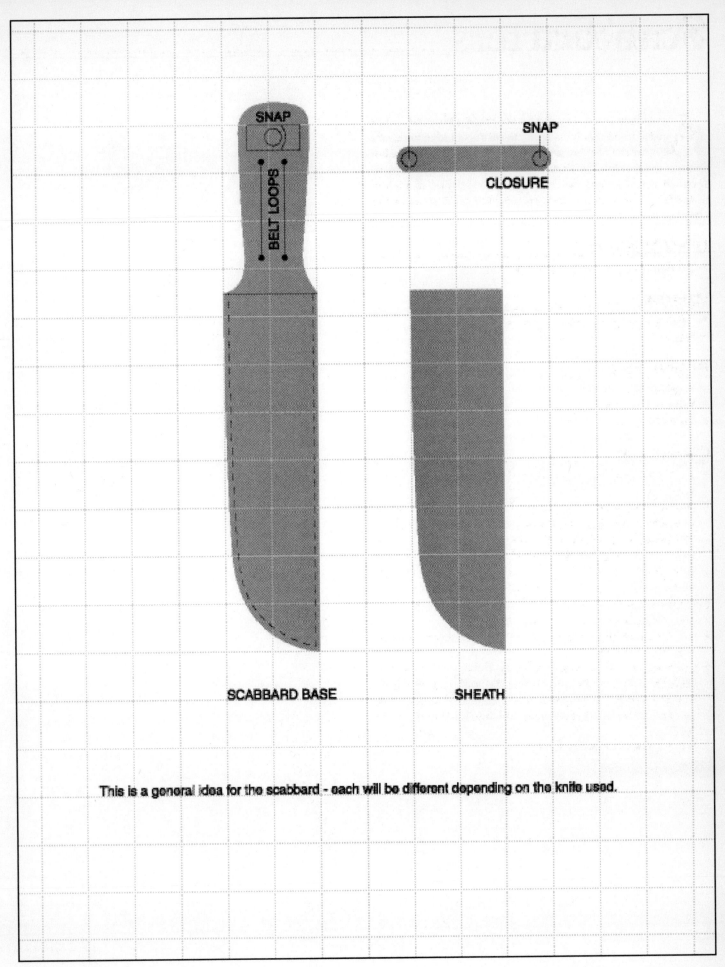

SNAP

BELT LOOPS

SNAP

CLOSURE

SCABBARD BASE

SHEATH

This is a general idea for the scabbard - each will be different depending on the knife used.

Pattern is 50% actual size.

Arm Garters

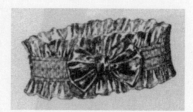

Garters were worn by the working classes around the upper arm to keep fullness of the sleeves up and out of the way of work. They were later worn to indicate the wearer's state of mourning or for identification. Use for barkeeps, clowns, or Dickensian working men.

Materials

- 1-inch ribbon
- ½-inch ribbon
- ½-inch elastic

Construction

- Measure the circumference of the arm around the bicep.
- For each garter, cut a piece of 1-inch ribbon and a piece of ½-inch ribbon, double the length of the measurement taken.
- Sew the ½-inch ribbon onto the middle of the 1-inch ribbon.
- Cut a piece of elastic the circumference of the arm, less one inch.
- Thread elastic through the ribbon.
- With right sides together, sew the ends closed through all layers.

Note: Leg garters would be made the same way—just use the measurement around the leg at whatever position you would like the garter to sit, instead of the arm measurement.

Domino Mask

Half masks, dominoes are worn for masquerades. During the 17th century, women and children wore these when traveling as protection against the sun and wind. This style of mask appears in many operas and could be used in *A Doll's House*, or for many of the commedia dell'arte plays.

Materials

- ¼ yard fabric
- Stitch Witchery
- Non-raveling fabric or felt for backing
- Ties or elastic

Pattern Pieces

- Mask (cut 1 fabric after bonding—see below)

Construction

- Following the instructions on page 3 enlarge pattern piece.
- Heat set face fabric to backing with the Stitch Witchery.
- Lay the pattern on the backing fabric and cut out mask. Double check that all the edges have been securely bonded.
- Topstitch close to all the cut edges.
- Add decorative trims as desired.
- Sew on elastic or ties at the sides as indicated.

Note: To make a sleeping mask, eliminate the eyeholes.

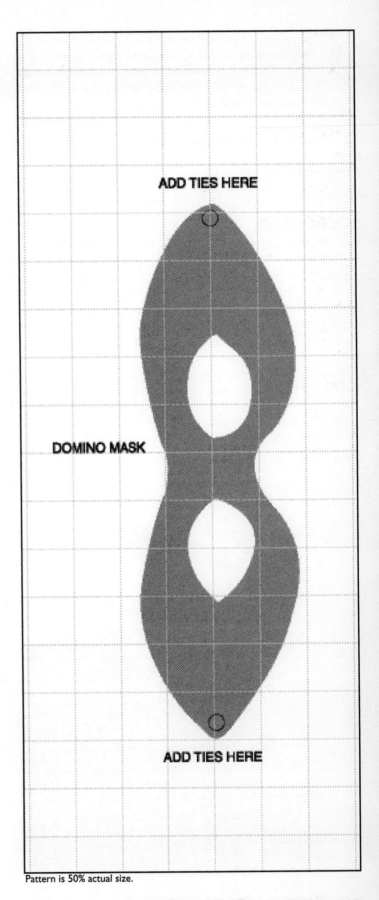

ADD TIES HERE

DOMINO MASK

ADD TIES HERE

Pattern is 50% actual size.

Zorro (Self Tie) Mask

The origins of masks in general can be traced back to antiquity but have evolved over time. This tied mask is named after the fictional character of television and movies; it may be worn by men in costume ball situations.

Materials

- ⅛ yard fabric, 45 inches wide

Pattern Pieces

- Mask (cut 1)

Construction

- Following the instructions on page 3, enlarge pattern piece and cut.
- On the backside, mark the eyeholes. Machine or hand stitch on the line.
- Cut out eyeholes. Either machine zigzag over the cut edge or hand sew using a blanket stitch.
- Hem all outer edges with a small rolled (shirt tail) hem.

Note: If using lightweight fabric, cut 2 adding seam allowances as desired. With right sides together, stitch around 3 sides, leaving 1 short end open through which to turn mask. Clip curves and corners. Turn right side out and stitch open end closed. Sew eyeholes as described above.

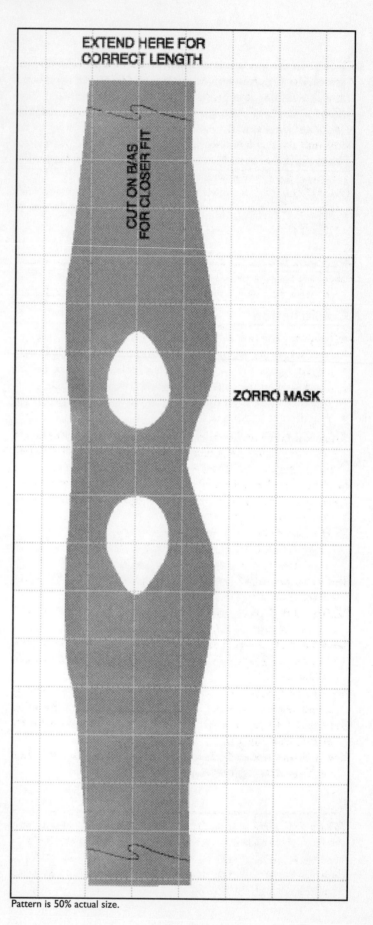

EXTEND HERE FOR CORRECT LENGTH

CUT ON BIAS FOR CLOSER FIT

ZORRO MASK

Pattern is 50% actual size.

Glossary of Costume/Clothing Terms

A

Accessories: Articles, worn or carried, that complete a costume, e.g., shoes, hats, jewelry, neckwear, belts, and scarves.

Apron: Garment of cloth, plastic, or leather worn over clothing to protect or adorn it.

Armband: Band of fabric worn around the upper arm, usually to show an affiliation with a group. A black armband is frequently worn on the sleeve during mourning.

Ascot: Neck scarf or tie with broad ends, tied so that one end falls over the other. Supposedly developed to wear at the Ascot horse races.

B

Babushka: Large trianglular scarf, or square scarf folded in half to form a triangle, worn over the head and tied under the chin.

Bag wig: Wig with a bag in the back to hold a ponytail and tied at the nape of the neck with a bow.

Baldric: (Baldrick) Belt, band or sash for decoration or usefulness—originally designed to support a sword or bugle. (Same as Bandoleer.)

Balmoral bonnet: Scottish cap of the tam-o'-shanter style with a round tip, often with a plaid band and a cockade or sprig of greenery.

Bandanna: Large neckerchief worn as decorative neck or headpiece. Originally a large brightly colored handkerchief with tie-dyed patterns, from Bandhnu, for this type of dying.

Bandoleer (or Bandolier): Broad band, belt or scarf worn over one shoulder and under the other. Originally worn as part of military dress.

Baseball cap: Cap worn by the players in a game of baseball. Usually a six-piece crown with a button on top and a stiff visor in the front to shield the eyes from the sun.

Beanie: Small round tight-fitting skullcap worn by schoolboys and college freshmen.

Bellhop or Bellboy cap: Pillbox hat, usually trimmed with braid or buttons, worn by hotel bellhops.

Beret (be-ray): Round soft cap adapted from the Basque beret; a visorless, usually woolen, cap with a tight headband and a soft full flat top.

Bib: 1). Small collar. 2). Piece of fabric worn over front of clothing as protection when eating. 3). Part of an apron above the waist.

Bonnet: Cloth or straw hat tied under the chin and worn by women and children.

Buster Brown collar: Wide starched collar worn with a Windsor tie. Named for a comic strip character of the 1900s.

C

Calotte (ka-lot): Greek skullcap worn by all classes, later a small round cap worn under a priest's hood to cover the tonsure hairstyle. A small close fitting sectional cap. (Also calot, callot.)

Caul (cawl): Net holding hair in place on the back of the head (Greek through Middle-Ages). A type of snood.

Chaperone: Ancient type of hood covering head and shoulders. Worn by men and women from Middle Ages through the Renaissance.

Charlotte Corday cap: Soft mobcap, longer in the back than front, with ruffle framing the face. Worn by Charlotte Corday (1769-1793) who was guillotined during the French Revolution.

Chefs hat: Hat worn by chefs and others in the food service business. Usually a band with a large circular puffed or pleated top.

Coif: Close fitting cap fastened with a tie under the chin.

Cravat [kra-vat]: Necktie folded or tied at front with ends tucked inside garment. First found in the 17th century.

Cravat string: Ribbon used to tie a heavy 17th century lace cravat in place.

Cuff: 1) Band or fold at the end of a sleeve, either sewn on or detachable. 2) Turned up fold at the bottom of a trouser leg.

Cummerbund: Broad waistband usually worn in place of a vest with men's dress clothes and adapted in various styles for women's clothes.

D

Deerstalker: See fore and aft cap.

Diadem: Tiara or small, jeweled crown.

Domino: 1) Mask, especially half mask worn for masquerades. 2) Mask worn by women and children in the 17th century as protection against sun and wind.

Driving cap: Sporting cap with a flat crown and a front visor. Modern term for the 1950s style golf cap.

Duffel bag: Sturdy cylindrical bag originally carried by sailors and other military personnel for transporting clothing and personal belongings. Usually made of waterproof canvas or duck.

E

Envelope bag: Handbag with a flap closing, as on an envelope.

Epaulet (also-epaulette): Shoulder trimming, usually a band secured with a button.

Eton cap: A small brimmed, four- or six-section beanie worn by boys at Eton College, England.

F

Falling band collar: Wide collar, turned down over shoulders, usually linen or fine fabric often lace trimmed. Worn by men in the 17th Century after the accession of Charles I in 1625. Also Van Dyke Collar.

Fan collar: Frilly standing collar, high at back of neck and flared in the form of a fan.

Fichu (fish-oo): Draped scarf or shawl, worn around shoulders, knotted at breast and ends hanging. Also Fichu.

Fore-and-aft cap: A cap with a visor front and back. (Also deerstalker, Sherlock Holmes cap.)

Four-in-hand: A kind of necktie tied with a slipknot. This tie became popular for the first time in the 1870s.

G

Gaiter: Cloth or leather covering for ankle or leg closed up the side. Often secured with a strap under the ankle.

Garter: Band worn around knee to keep stockings up or around arm to hold sleeve in a shortened position.

Gauntlet: 1) Glove with wrist section that covers part of the arm. 2) Glove worn with ancient armor. 3) That part of any glove covering part of the wrist.

Gladstone collar: Standing collar with points flaring out at the side front. Worn with silk scarf tie. Named for William Ewart Gladstone, Prime Minister of England.

Glove: Covering for the hand that has separate sheaths for each finger, distinguishing it from a mitt or a mitten.

Golf cap: Man's sport cap with round flat top, fitted headband and visor.

H

Hanger sword: Sword worn from a waist belt, usually under the coat.

Hoover collar: Man's shirt collar with rounded corners falling from a rise. Often made of paper or starched linen and detachable.

J

Jabot (zhah- bo): 1) Fall of lace or cloth attached to the front of a neckband and worn by men in the 18th century. 2) Pleated frill of cloth or lace attached down the center front of a woman's blouse or dress.

Juliet cap: Small, close fitting cap of lace, net or mesh, usually decorated with pearls or gems.

L

Lappet: Lace, linen, or ribbon piece that hangs from the side or back of a headpiece.

Liripipe: Long tail on a hood.

M

Miser's Purse: Made of a tube of material, often a net, with a metal ring that slides down to close the opening.

Mitre [my-ter]: Tall peaked liturgical headdress worn by bishops, the Pope, and abbots in the Catholic Church as a sign of office.

Mitt: Fingerless glove.

Mitten: Covering for the hand and wrist having a separate section for the thumb only.

Mob cap: Women's cap or headdress with full crown, usually soft.

Moufles: Fingerless gloves worn by workers or hunters. [Also Mitons.]

Muff: Cylindrical shaped object, covered with fur or other material, into which the hands are placed from either end to keep them warm.

N

Newsboys cap: Cap consisting of a large pieced crown and a small visor, typically worn by boys who sold newspapers around the turn of the 20th century.

Night cap: Cap worn to bed to keep the head warm or to keep hair in place.

O

Overseas cap: Olive drab (later khaki) wool cap having no visor or stiffening, worn by the U.S. Army during WWI and WWII. Sometimes called an envelope cap.

P

Peter Pan collar: Flat shaped collar, with round corners, highly popular in the 1950s. This collar was named, in the 1900s, for the title character of Peter Pan by James M. Barrie, as worn by Maude Adams.

Pill box hat: Cap with straight sides and a flat top.

Pinafore: Overdress/apron. Originally worn over a blouse or dress to protect dresses from dirt and later adapted for fashion.

Pocket: Small bag used to carry money or piece of fabric applied to a garment to create a container.

Pocket square: Decorative handkerchief for wearing in a man's suit jacket or sport coat pocket. May be a actual square or just the visible points attached to a card.

Q

Quiver: Case for holding arrows.

R

Rabat: Turned down collar falling over the shoulders worn by gentlemen in the 15th and 16th centuries. Also a clerical collar, sometimes having two short breast pieces.

Reticule: Small drawstring purse.

Ruff: Wheel shaped, pleated collar, made of stiff starched linen or muslin and frequently trimmed with lace, worn in the 16th and 17th centuries. Said to have been introduced by Catherine de Medici, circa 1500. In style through the 1620s.

S

Saddlebag: Pair of covered pouches laid across the back of a horse behind the saddle.

Sailor collar: Faced collar, square in back narrowing to a V in front. Styled after American sailors. Often trimmed with braid and a knot in front, or a scarf worn underneath.

Santa Claus hat: Pointed cap with fur band and a bell or pompon on the end, usually red.

Sash: Ornamental band or scarf worn around the body.

Scabbard: Sheath or case to hold the blade of a knife or sword.

Shoe tongue: Strip of leather at the throat of the shoe, extending up above the buckles or lacings. Decorated in the 17th and 18th centuries.

Skullcap: Small close fitting cap covering only the crown of the head. Originally made of iron and sewn inside a cap for protection.

Sleeve garter: A band worn around the arm to hold up a too-long sleeve, or to keep the sleeve out of the way while working.

Slipper: Any footwear lower than the ankle, usually without a means of fastening—"slip" on the foot.

Snood: Baglike net worn at the back of the head to hold hair.

Spats: Short cloth gaiter worn over shoes by men and women. Short for spatterdash.

Spatterdash: Cover for leg, similar to legging or gaiter. Worn to protect stockings against mud.

Steinkirk: A scarf of lace or lawn, loosely tied with the ends twisted in to the vest front or drawn through a buttonhole.

Stock: A high, stiffened collar band, fastened in the back with strings or buckles (called stock buckles).

T

Tam-o'-shanter: Round flat cap with a tight fitting headband.

Tiara: 1) Woman's crown-like headdress of flowers or jewels. 2) Coronet. 3) The Pope's triple crown.

Tip: Top of the crown of a hat.

Tudor Beret: Henry VIII hat. [Also Renaissance beret.]

V

Van Dyke collar: See falling band collar.

Visor: Front brim of a cap for shading the eyes from the sun.

W

Windsor tie: Large flowing bowtie of the 1870s and 80s; a 19th century version of the late 17th century cravat.

Wing collar: Man's standing collar with corners folded down giving wing like effect. Worn with full dress and formal daytime dress.

Y

Yarmulke: Skullcap often worn by Jewish men and boys.

Z

Zucchetto: (zoo-ket-oh) Skullcap worn by the Roman Catholic clergy. A beanie.

Glossary of Sewing/Fabric Terms

A

Abbot cloth: Heavy basket woven drapery material, usually cotton.

Acetate: Generic term for a manmade fiber often used in blends with other fibers.

Acrylic: Generic term for a manmade fiber, often used with natural fibers to make wool-like fabrics and knitted goods.

Alpaca: Fabric made from soft, strong fibers from the long hair of Peruvian alpaca. It is classified as wool.

Angora: Fabric made from soft smooth hair of the Angora goat, or the fine hair of the Angora rabbit; also known as Mohair. It is classified as wool.

Antique satin: Heavy dull-faced satin.

Appliqué: Separate motif or design applied onto the face of a fabric.

B

Back: The under or wrong side of a fabric; opposite of the face.

Bag lining: Stitching a lining layer around the outside of a piece and turning through to encase the raw edge(s).

Basting: Long, loose temporary stitch used in the preparatory phase of sewing to hold two or more pieces together.

Batiste: Sheer cotton, linen, or synthetic fabric of a plain weave.

Bengaline: Woven fabric with pronounced crosswise ribs, sometimes called faille.

Bias: Diagonal direction of fabric. True bias is at a 45-degree angle to the grainline.

Bias binding: Narrow strip of material cut on the bias, or diagonal weave of the fabric, with the edges folded in ready to apply. Used to encase edges as a finish or trim.

Binding: Strip encasing edges as finish or trim.

Blind hem: Hem sewn invisibly with hand stitches or on a blind hem machine.

Blanket stitch: Decorative hand stitch used along the outer seam or raw edge of an item, used to keep the fabric from fraying. Working from left to right with the edges of the fabric facing you, start as you would a whip stitch, bringing the needle up through the fabric, but before you pull the thread taut, bring your needle down through the stitch to create a small half knot or "bead". Carefully set each stitch a set distance apart.

Bobbinet: Fine machine-made net with hexagonal mesh.

Bonding: Joining two or more layers together with glue or heat.

Boning: Pieces, originally of bone and later of steel, wood, or plastic, used to stiffen seams, edges, or structural lines of a garment. Can be flexible or not depending on the substance used.

Boucle [boo-klay]: Woven or knitted fabric with a nubbly texture, made of looped fibers.

Bound seam: Seam edge bound with bias binding.

Box-pleat: Combination of two flat folds in opposite directions with turned under edges meeting underneath.

Braid: Narrow flat trim, usually woven or braided.

Brim: Extended rim of a hat.

Broadcloth: Closely woven fabric with very small crosswise ribs. Made in many weights, fibers. and blends.

Brocade: Jacquard weave fabric with raised interwoven patterns, often emphasized with gold or silver threads.

Buckram: Coarse linen or cotton cloth stiffened with paste or gum. Commonly used for hat construction.

Burlap: Coarse and heavy plain weave fabric made of jute, hemp, or cotton.

C

Calico: Fabric, usually cotton or cotton blend, in a plain weave and typically with a small printed pattern, most often floral.

Cambric: Fine closely woven white or yarn-dyed cotton fabric in plain weave with a slight gloss on the right side. Also historically called cotton cambric or cambric muslin.

Canvas: Heavy strong plain-woven fabric of cotton, linen, silk, or a blend. (From the Latin cannabis meaning hemp.)

Cap-mesh: Open weave plastic or synthetic fabric used for the ventilated backs of modern baseball caps. Semi-stiff, comes in a number of colors.

Cashmere: Fabric made from the soft hair of a Kashmir goat.

Castellated: An edging that looks like the square notched top of a castle.

Challis [shal'-ee]: Soft lightweight fabric usually printed with a design. May be wool, rayon, cotton, or a blend.

Chambray: Fine quality plain weave fabric with a linen-like finish.

Charmeuse [shar-mooz]: Soft lightweight fabric in a satin weave with a twilled back and a soft luster. Used for draped dresses and under garments. May be made of silk, rayon, or synthetic fibers.

Chenille: Fabric woven with soft tufts.

Chevron: V-shaped stripes.

Chiffon: Delicate, soft, transparent fabric in plain weave. Usually made of silk, rayon, or polyester.

China silk: Thin, plain weave silk, usually used for lining.

Chintz: Highly glazed cotton with a shiny finish.

Clip: Cut into fabric to allow ease on curves or corners.

Cloqué (Clokey or Cloky): From the French for blistered, fabrics with irregular raised surface texture. Similar to mattelasse.

Closure: Devise that opens or closes a garment, such as buttons, or the area on which they are placed.

Corduroy: Cotton or rayon cut pile fabric in either plain or twill weave with wide or narrow wales (cords or ribs) which are formed by extra weft or filling.

Cotton: Fabric made of fibers from the seedpods of a cotton plant.

Coutil (coo-till or coo-tee): Sturdy fabric of cotton, woven in a herringbone or jacquard weave. Used for corsets

Crepe: Fabric with a pebbly, crinkled, or puckered finish. May be any fiber but most usually silk, rayon or polyester.

Crepe-back-satin: Fabric with a satin finish on the face and crepe on the back.

Crinoline: Open stiff weave fabric used as a foundation for supporting a skirt. Usually made of stiffened silk, cotton, or synthetic fiber.

D

Dagged edge: Edge finished with pointed triangular shapes.

Damask: Silk or linen fabric with a woven pattern which is reversed on the opposite side. Named for Damascus, where the fabric originated, it was first brought to the western world by Marco Polo in the 13th century.

Denim: Coarse, strong, washable cotton in twill weave of dyed yarn woven sometimes with white, sometimes with different colored fillings. From the French de nimes after the town of Nimes.

Double fold bias tape: Strip of bias-cut fabric with the edges folded to the wrong side, meeting in the center, and then folded again just off center. Used to encase seams, size is designated by the folded width. (1/2 inch double fold is made from a 2-inch bias strip.)

Double knit: Woolen or synthetic fibers knitted on two sets of needles, creating a durable fabric with a double thickness.

Drill: Twilled linen or cotton fabric.

Duck: Durable, heavy, tightly woven fabric usually of cotton or linen, made of various weights in plain or rib weaves.

E

Easing: Working extra fullness into a seam, often with the use of a gathering stitch.

Edgestitch: Topstitching placed very close to finished edge.

Embroidery: Ornamental needlework done on fabric in either the same or contrasting colors.

Enclosed seams: Seams concealed by two garment layers.

Eyelet: Fabric with small decorative holes or perforations.

Eyelet embroidery: Openwork embroidery, same as Madeira embroidery.

F

Face: The side of the fabric that is intended to be seen.

Facing: Fabric applied to garment edge, usually on the underside, used as a substitute for a hem or for lining parts of a garment.

Fagoting: Decorative stitch used to join two fabric sections that are spread apart.

Faille [fyle]: Slightly glossy fabric in a ribbed weave with crosswise grain or heavier threads or heavy fill yarns.

Felt: Non-woven fabric, originally wool, fur, or mohair, now often synthetic.

Fiber: Fundamental unit used in the production of fabric.

Finger press: Pressing a small area with your fingers rather than an iron. This produces a softer press line.

Flannel: Soft lightweight fabric slightly napped on one side in plain or twill weave, usually wool or cotton.

Flat felled seam: Flat seam with both raw edges encased. Looks the same on right and wrong sides. Very sturdy finish.

Flat lining: A second layer of fabric stitched onto the back of a pattern piece in order to add stability.

French seam: A seam made by stitching the seam on the right sides of the fabric, trimming the seam down, and re-stitching on the wrong side of the fabric and encasing the raw edges.

G

Gabardine: 1) Firm twilled worsted fabric with diagonal rib weave on one side. 2) Softer fabric of various fibers with raised ribs on right side.

Gather: To pull fabric along a line of stitching so as to draw it into puckers.

Georgette: Sheer soft crepe, heavier than chiffon.

Gingham: Plain weave fabric with two colors creating a checked pattern. Usually woven of cotton or a blend.

Godet: Triangular piece of cloth set into a garment for fullness or decoration.

Gore: Tapered section of garment, wider at lower edge.

Grain: Direction in which the threads composing the fabric run. The lengthwise grain follows the warp, the crosswise grain follows the weft.

Grommet: Metal eyelet.

Grosgrain [groh'-grayn]: Fabric or, most commonly, ribbon having heavy crosswise ribs. Used for headsize bands inside hats and for decorative trimming.

Gusset: 1) Shaped fabric piece inserted in a garment, glove, or shoe to give additional strength or room. 2) Piece of chain or plate mail at joint openings in ancient armor.

H

Hem: Finish for the end of a piece of fabric made by folding the end over, then over itself again, concealing the first turn.

Hemp: Coarse, tough fiber of the hemp plant, used for weaving into textural fabrics.

Hook and loop tape: Generic term for Velcro.

Horsehair/horsehair braid: Stiff bias braid woven of synthetic fiber, available in different widths and colors and used to stiffen hem edges, to maintain a shape (as inside bows or ribbon loops) or attached to the inside of a hat or cap allowing it to be pinned to the actor's hair or wig.

I

Illusion: Type of tulle, originally made of silk, used for veils, dresses, and trims.

Inset: Fabric section or trim inserted within garment for fit or decoration.

Interlining: Layer of fabric placed between garment and underlining for warmth.

Interlock: Knit fabric with the same look on either side, often used for T-shirts.

J

Jacquard [ja-kard]: Weave that produces woven designs on both sides of the fabric, named after the inventor of the loom that first produced this type of fabric.

Jersey: Plain knit of natural or synthetic fibers producing a soft pliable fabric.

L

Lamé: Fabric woven with a metallic thread, often brocaded. Sometimes mixed with silk or other fiber.

Lap: Any edge that extends over another edge, as on a placket.

Lawn: Fine, soft sheer fabric, usually cotton, in plain weave and starched or stiffened.

Leno: 1) Type of weave with paired and twisted warp threads. 2) Loose open fabric woven in this style.

Linen: Strong lustrous fabric woven of smooth textured flax, usually in plain weave but often damask.

Lining: Material that lines or that is used to line the inner surface of a garment.

M

Matelasse: Soft fabric with raised woven designs in quilted or irregular patterns, having a blistered finish. Woven of almost any fiber combination.

Melton: Thick heavy woven material with a smooth sheared surface, usually wool or wool blend. Used primarily for overcoats and jackets.

Middy braid: Narrow finely ribbed flat braid, originally used to trim naval middy blouses.

Moire: Usually silk fabric with a waved or watered pattern and often ribbed or corded. It is produced by rolling the fabric between engraved cylinders, which crush designs into the fabric.

Monks cloth: A heavy basket weave cloth used for draperies.

Muslin: Plain weave fabric of cotton, bleached or unbleached. The weight of the fibers can vary, creating different weights and thickness. Also the term used for a mock-up costume.

N

Nap: Soft surface fibers that lie smoothly in one direction.

Notch: 1) Pattern symbol transferred to fabric to indicate matching points. 2) To cut wedges out of the seam allowance.

Nylon: Highly elastic, very strong synthetic material made into thread and then woven or knit into yardage. The resulting fabric is machine washable.

O

Organdy: Crisp, sheer, plain weave cotton, may be solid or over-embroidered.

Organza: Sheer, fine crisp fabric, usually silk or synthetic.

Osnaburg: Coarse woven heavy cloth originally of linen, now of cotton. Used for making sacks and work clothes.

Ottoman: Firm, plain heavy fabric with crossgrain flat ribs.

Overcast stitch: Slanted stitch used to prevent raw edges from raveling or to hold two edges together.

Overlock: Machine overcast stitch done by a multiple thread machine such as a serger or Merrow® machine

P

Passementerie: Trimming, particularly heavy embroideries or edgings.

Peau de soie [poh-deh-swah]: French, meaning silk skin. Soft silk or man-made fiber in a satin weave.

Pelt: Skin of animal with fur intact.

Petersham: Heavy corded ribbon, used for inner belts, hatbands and hat trimmings. Also called French belting. Similar to grosgrain.

Pin-baste: Temporarily hold with pins as in basting.

Pinking: Cutting raw edge with pinking or scalloping shears to prevent raveling.

Pique: Cotton with a raised woven pattern, either corded or birdseye.

Placket: Garment opening that may be fastened with zipper, snaps, buttons, or hooks and eyes.

Plain weave: The simplest of weaves; each weft thread goes alternately over and under each warp thread, producing a flat even surface.

Pleat: Fold of fabric laid flat back on itself, arranged singularly or in groups or the process of arranging the folds.

Pleather: Artificial leather.

Plisse [plee-say]: Cotton fabric that has been chemically shrunk in lines to create a rippled effect; from the French, meaning crinkled or pleated.

Pongee: Natural, nubby silk, usually a tan color.

Poplin: Heavy weight cotton with a very fine rib running selvage to selvage.

Polyester: Trade name referring to a specific, or generic name referring to any, man-made fiber. Fabric woven or knitted from these fibers is very durable and wrinkle resistant.

Q

Quilting: Fabric construction with a layer of padding placed between two layers of fabric and then held in place with decorative stitching.

R

Ramie: Natural fiber similar to flax. When woven or knit, it looks like linen.

Raw edge: Unfinished edge of fabric.

Rayon: Any of various textile fibers synthetically produced by pressing a cellulose solution through very small holes and solidifying it into filaments.

Rigelene: Synthetic boning composed of multiple strands of stiff polyester fiber in a woven casing.

Right side: The outside, finished side of a garment or piece of fabric.

Rolled Hem: A very narrow hem made by gently rolling the edge of the fabric and slip stitching the roll.

Rosette: Ribbon decoration formed of loops, usually in the shape of a rose.

Running Stitch: A series of short stitches of the same length taken on the needle at one time. Used for seaming, gathering, tucking, and quilting.

S

Sateen: Smooth shiny cotton woven to imitate satin.

Satin: A basic weave in which a shiny weft thread passes over three or four warp threads, producing a fabric with a lustrous surface. Also the name of the fabric produced by this weaving.

Seam: Joining line where pieces of fabric are sewn together.

Seam allowance: Width of fabric beyond seam line.

Seam binding: Ribbon-like tape used to finish edges.

Selvage: Lengthwise finished edges of all woven fabrics.

Shank: Link between button and fabric to allow for thickness of overlapping fabric.

Shantung: Silk fabric of plain weave with an irregular surface due to slubs and variations in the thickness of the threads.

Shirt tail hem: Small double fold hem, used on a contemporary man's shirt.

Silk: Filaments produced by silkworms and then woven into a variety of fabrics or the name for any of these fabrics.

Single fold bias tape: Strip of bias fabric with edges folded to the wrong side and meeting in the center. The measurement on the package is the width of the front surface once the folds are put in.

Slipstitch: Loose stitches concealed between two thicknesses of fabric. Made by taking up thread of fabric then running needle through fold of hem.

Sole: Bottom piece of any kind of footwear, the part underneath the wearer's foot.

Soutache: Narrow braid trim.

Stay stitch: Stitching used to give fabric extra stability and shape as you assemble a garment. Stay stitching is sewn inside the seam allowance while the pieces are flat. It can act as a guide for clipping a curve or to prevent stretching.

Stitch Witchery: Thin web of glue, in sheet form, used to bond two materials together.

Suede: Leather, usually calf, finished by buffing the flesh side to produce a napped surface.

Swiss mesh: Sheer woven fabric of nylon, polyester, or other synthetic fiber. The scale runs from very coarse, almost like door screening, to very fine, almost like organza.

T

Tack: To hold layers of fabric together at a single point.

Taffeta: Smooth gloss silk or synthetic fabric in a plain weave alike on both sides; fine but with a lot of body. (First used in the 16th century)

Tapestry: Fabric with colors woven in with colored weft threads. Also Jacquard weave fabrics imitating original handwoven tapestries.

Tip: Top of the crown of a hat.

Tobacco cloth: Nautral, loosely woven gauzy fabric. Used to shade tobacco while growing. Good for peasant shirts and scarves.

Topstitching: Machine stitching on the right side of a garment, parallel to a seam or edge.

Tulle: Thin fine netting, now most often of polyester, although silk and cotton are still being made. Used for tutus, veils, etc.

Tweed: Formerly all wool, homespun fabric from Scotland. Now, rough surfaced wool or wool blend fabrics with a homespun effect.

Twill: A weave that produces diagonal lines or ribs. Also fabric woven in this manner.

Twill tape: Firmly woven tape used in tailoring to reinforce seams and for casings. Can be cotton, linen, nylon or poly-blend.

U

Ultra-suede: Washable synthetic suede.

V

Velvet: Fabric with short, thick soft pile of looped warp yarns and plain back

Velveteen: Woven pile fabric similar to velvet, but with a visibly shorter nap.

Voile: A fine, soft plain weave fabric, usually of cotton. It is less transparent than chiffon.

W

Whipstitch: Overcast stitch used to hold two finished edges together or a separate piece onto the garment as with an appliqué. Needle goes in perpendicular to the edge, and stitches are evenly spaced with a uniform depth.

Wonder-Under: A two-part bonding used for appliqué work. The glue web is bonded to the wrong side of the appliqué motif or fabric. The paper backing is then removed and the appliqué is heat bonded to the base.

Wool: Probably the oldest of the natural fibers, it comes from a variety of animals including sheep, goats and camels and is spun into a large variety of weights and woven or knit into an untold number of different fabrics.

Y

Yoke: Fitted portion of a garment usually over shoulders or hips to which the rest of the garment is sewn.

Measurement Sheet _____

Name _____

Height _____	Waist to thigh _____
Weight _____	to knee _____
Chest _____	to ankle _____
Waist _____	to floor _____
Hips _____	
Under bust _____	
Underbust to waist _____	Inseam _____
Shoulders (both) _____	Crotch _____
(one) _____	Thigh _____
	Knee above _____
Arm Length to elbow	Knee below _____
outside _____	
inside _____	Head _____
	Neck base _____
Bicep _____	Neck middle _____
Forearm _____	
Wrist _____	
Armscye _____	Shoe _____
Width of chest	Dress or suit _____
front _____	Shirt or blouse _____
back _____	Bra _____
Neck to waist	Pants _____
front _____	Hat _____
back _____	Glove _____
Shoulder to bust _____	
Shoulder to waist _____	Allergies _____
Width of bust _____	Ears piereced _____
Underarm to waist _____	

Bibliography

Barton, Lucy. *Historic Costumes for the Stage*. Boston: Walter H Baker Co. 1963

Baumgarten, Linda and John Watson with Florice Carr. *Costume Close up*. New York: Costume & Fashion Press, 1999.

Beardsley, Aubrey. *Aubrey Beardsley Drawings*. New York: United Book Guild, 1967.

Blum, Stella. *Ackermann's Costume Plates, Women's Fashions in England, 1818-1828*. New York: Dover Publications, Inc., 1978.

———. *Everyday Fashions of the Thirties as Pictured in Sears Catalogs*. New York: Dover Publications, Inc.,1986.

———. *Everyday Fashions of the Twenties as Pictured in Sears and Other Catalogs*. New York... Dover Publications, Inc.,1981.

Boucher, Francois. *20,000 Years of Fashion. The History of Costume and Personal Adornment*. New York: Harry N. Abrams, Inc.

Bradfield, Nancy. *Costume In Detail*. New York: Costume and Fashion Press 1968, 1981.

Bradley, Caroline. *Western World Costume: An Outline History*. New York, Appleton-Century Crofts, Inc. 1954.

Braun & Schneider. *Historic Costumes in Pictures*. New York: Dover Publications Inc.,1975.

Butler Brothers. *Men's and Boys Wear, Dept G Catalog*. Baltimore, Maryland. Issued June 30, 1947.

Cabarga, Leslie. *Popular Advertising Cuts of the Twenties and Thirties*. New York: Dover Publications, Inc. 1996.

Colle, Doriece. *Collars. Stocks .Cravats*. Pennsylvania: Rodale Press, Inc. 1972.

Cunnington, Phillis and Catherine Lucas. *Costume for Births, Marriages & Deaths*. London: Adam & Charles Black Limited, 1972.

Delineator an Illustrated Magazine of Literature and Fashion, Vol. LXI No. for January 1903. New York: The Butterick Publishing Company, Limited, 1902

Dreher, Denise. *From The Neck Up*. Minneapolis: Madhatter Press, 1981.

Druesedow, Jean L. *Men's Fashion Illustration from the Turn of the Century*. Dover Publications, Inc., 1990.

Gimbel Brothers. *Gimbel's Illustrated 1915 Fashion Catalog*. New York: Dover Publication, Inc., 1994.

Grafton, Carol Belanger. *Fashions of the Thirties: 476 Authentic Copyright-Free Illustrations*. New York: Dover Publications, Inc. 1993.

———. *Old-Fashioned Illustrations of Books, Reading and Writing*. New York: Dover Publications, Inc., 1992.

———. *Shoes, Hats and Fashion Accessories: A Pictorial Archive 1850-1940*. New York: Dover Publications, Inc., 1998.

———. *Trades and Occupations. A Pictorial Archive From Early Sources*. New York: Dover Publications, Inc., 1990.

Harter, Jim. *Men: A Pictorial Archive From Nineteenth Century Sources*. New York: Dover Publications, Inc., 1980.

———. *Women: A Pictorial Archive From Nineteenth Century Sources*. New York: Dover Publications, Inc., 1982.

Klepper, Erhard. *Costume through the Ages*. New York: Dover Publications, Inc., 1999.

Kunciov, Robert, editor. *Mr. Godey's Ladies*. New York: Bonanza Books, 1971.

Livoni, Philip, editor. *Russell's Standard Fashions 1915-1919*. New York: Dover Publications, Inc., 1996.

Mitchell Co., Jno. J. *Men's Fashion Illustrations from The Turn of the Century*. New York: Dover Publications, Inc., 1990.

Montgomery, David. *Native American Crafts & Skills*. New York: The Lyons Press, 2000. [Originally published in 1985 by Horizon Publishers.]

Mulari, Mary. *Mary Mulari's Accessories With Style*. Iola, Wisconsin: Krause Publications, 2001.

National Cloak and Suit Company. *The National Style Book*, Vol. 18, No. 4. New York, 1914.

National Cloak and Suit Company. *The National Style Book*, Vol. 19, No. 2. New York, 1915.

Olian, JoAnne, editor. *Authentic French Fashion Plates of the Twenties*. New York: Dover Publications, Inc., 1990.

———. *Everyday Fashions of the Forties as Pictured in Sears Catalogs*. New York: Dover Publications, Inc., 1992.

Peacock, John. *Fashion Accessories: The Complete 20th Century Sourcebook*. London: Thames & Hudson Ltd., 2000.

Picken, Mary Brooks. *The Fashion Dictionary*. New York: Funk & Wagnall's, 1957.

Sears, Roebuck and Co. Catalogue No.117, 1908.

———. Catalog Fall and Winter, 1927.

The Vogue Company. *Vogue*, Vol. 47, No.8. New York, April 15, 1916.

Vogue Sewing New York: The Butterick Publishing Co., 2000.

Waugh, Norah. *Corsets and Crinolines*. New York: Theatre Arts Books, 1970.

———. *The Cut Of Men's Clothes*. London: Farber and Farber Limited, 1964.

Wilcox, R. Turner. *The Mode in Hats and Headress*. New York, London: Charles Scribner's Sons, 1959.
Page   Description

List of Illustrations _____

Authors' photo by Christine A. Butler.